more

knitting in the sun

32 PATTERNS TO KNIT FOR KIDS

DISCARD

more

knitting in the sun

32 PATTERNS TO KNIT FOR KIDS

BY KRISTI PORTER

WILEY

Wiley Publishing, Inc.

More Knitting in the Sun: 32 Patterns to Knit for Kids

Copyright © 2011 by Wiley Publishing, Inc., Hoboken, New Jersey. All rights reserved.

Published by Wiley Publishing, Inc., Hoboken, New Jersey

For general information on our other products and services or to obtain technical support please contact our Customer Care Department within the U.S. at (877) 762-2974, outside the U.S. at (317) 572-3993 or fax (317) 572-4002.

Wiley also publishes its books in a variety of electronic formats. Some content that appears in print may not be available in electronic books. For more information about Wiley products, please visit our web site at www.wiley.com.

Library of Congress Control Number: 2011922783

ISBN: 978-0-470-87448-6 (pbk)

ISBN: 978-1-118-07589-0 (ebk)

Printed in the United States of America

10 9 8 7 6 5 4 3 2 1

Book production by Wiley Publishing, Inc., Composition Services

credits

senior editor
Roxane Cerda

project editor
Carol Pogoni

editorial manager
Christina Stambaugh

vice president and publisher
Cindy Kitchel

vice president and executive publisher
Kathy Nebenhaus

interior design
Beth Brooks
Jennifer Mayberry

cover design
Wendy Mount

photography
Stephen Simpson

acknowledgments

They say that you can never step in the same river twice, and while it is certainly true that writing this book has differed from creating its predecessor, *Knitting in the Sun,* I've certainly enjoyed getting my feet wet once again! It is a pleasure to work again with many people who are now trusted and familiar friends. The editorial staff, the photographer, and the creators of over half of the designs in this book were also part of the original *Knitting in the Sun.* But creating this book has also afforded me the opportunity to get to know some new people and witness their creativity. So to all these friends, old and new, it's a privilege to be able to offer my heartfelt thanks here!

To the able folks at Wiley Publishing for putting this book together and bringing it out into the world, most especially my editors Roxane Cerda and Carol Pogoni, who continue to surprise me with their savvy, wisdom, and guidance. What a joy to work with people who regularly exceed my expectations!

To the designers who have made such great designs for kids to wear in warm weather. I appreciate their hard work, their thoughtfulness, and their thoroughness in creating patterns that will truly appeal to children—and the knitters who love them!

To my support team: my faithful knitters at Knitting in La Jolla, my kindred spirits of the Stitch Cooperative, and of course, my family. I am thankful every day that you make it possible to do the work that I love.

To the models who bring these designs to life on the page: Ana, Audrey, Cami, Croix, Danielle, Ella, Esmé, Jack, Julia, Kaylie, Lucca, Maddie, Maren, Monaghan, Noa, and Sophie. Shooting the photos, as you can see, was a lot of high-energy fun! I also want to thank their parents for being part of our occasionally chaotic process.

I am so pleased to work again with the wonderful photographer, Stephen Simpson. Doing the photography was literally a neighborhood project. All the photos were shot within walking distance of my house with neighborhood kids barefoot and laughing on warm summer evenings. That's what I remember, and, I think, what captures the spirit of the book—patterns for things real kids can wear on warm days and have fun in.

To all of you, my sincere thanks and gratitude!

76

80

86

91

96

101

108

113

117

124

128

134

138

149

156

164

table of contents

introduction

Knitting for kids is no easy feat. Add warm weather to the mix and you've really got yourself a challenge!

Kids want knits that aren't too babyish, but aren't miniature versions of adult designs either. They want clothes that are comfortable and easy to wear. Kids need to run and jump and play without fussing with their clothes. But they still want things that suit their own personal style, whether they are a girly girl or a hundred percent boy. But, compared to other age groups, there aren't many patterns specifically geared toward school-age kids. And if you've got to throw out the bulky pullovers, wooly hats, and mittens, your choices are even more limited!

smart design choices

I've sought out contributions from over twenty designers in order to bring together this collection of clothes and accessories for children between the ages of 2 and 12. I challenged them to come up with interesting, contemporary knits that are truly appropriate for kids in warmer climates. Since warm weather demands next-to-skin wear, I wanted easy pieces that can be layered and yarns that are light and cool. Cotton and cotton blends are obvious choices, but linen, hemp, bamboo, some great man-made blends, and even wool found their way into this book. The great news is that all the yarns used in this book are machine washable, so they can stand up to the demands of active kids and busy families. Looser gauges, lacy openwork, flowing shapes, and shortened sleeve lengths on cardigans and pullovers are some of the techniques that designers employed to create garments that will keep kids cool. These designs pay careful attention to straps and necklines so that kids stay covered even when they are on the go and so they won't constantly tug at their clothes. Fun accessories will make your child ready for any adventure.

Although this collection of knits is specifically designed for sunny days and warmer climates, it contains much more than summer clothes! For a climate like Southern California's, this book comprises a year-round wardrobe for a child. In places with genuine seasons, these designs will still see plenty of use. Children can wear these garments on their own in summertime or with a tee or turtleneck in cooler weather since most of the pieces are suitable for layering. And because these knits aren't bulky and the yarns aren't scratchy, you won't have to struggle getting your child to wear a coat on top.

how to use this book

The patterns in this book are sized to fit kids sizes 2–12. Because people come in all shapes and sizes, your child's age might not correspond to his/her size (just like when you buy clothing at a store). However, since it's much more work to re-knit a cardigan than it is to return one to the mall, be thoughtful when choosing the size to knit! The patterns in More Knitting in the Sun use the sizing standards created by the Craft Yarn Council of America (www.craftyarncouncil.com/childsize.html). Measure your child's chest circumference and knit the size appropriate for that measurement. If your child is shorter or taller than average you may wish to alter the length of the body or sleeves on a garment. A schematic of the finished measurements accompanies the garment patterns. To choose the best size, compare these measurements to a similar garment that fits your child well.

The patterns in this book cover a range of skill levels. Whether you are a new knitter or have a lifetime of knitting experience, you will find something to suit your abilities and taste for challenge. Use the information in the "Skills Used" section of each pattern to guide you. Knitting abbreviations and unusual techniques are described in the appendices in the back of the book.

Please take a moment to learn more about the wonderful designers whose patterns are featured in this book. You will find brief designer biographies as well as contact information for the companies that provided yarns for the projects in the back of the book.

Several of the patterns in this book rely on charts for stitch patterns and color work. Since knitters need to carry these charts with them and keep note of their progress, all the charts in this book are available as downloadable files at **www.wiley.com/go/moreknittinginthesun**. Updates or corrections to the information in this book will also be available at this website.

As a knitter, I know the feeling of pride I get when my girls wear something handknit. And I am so pleased to have gathered together this collection of knits that I truly believe will appeal to kids and keep you knitting for them year round. I hope this book will inspire you to knit for the children who bring sunshine into your lives every day of the year.

ACCESSORIES

JIM
beach cover-up

by janine le cras

This is the perfect hooded cover-up for your child to wear at the water's edge to keep the sun off or to provide protection against a chilly wind. It's knit in a soft superwash wool and organic cotton mix that is ideal for wearing next to the skin.

pattern notes

The body is knit in one piece from the front hem, divided at the neck, and rejoined to knit down the back. Stitches are picked up around the neck to knit the hood.

For instructions on picking up stitches and working a three-needle bind-off, please refer to the "Special Knitting Techniques" appendix.

seed stitch

(worked over an even number of sts)

Row 1: *K1, p1, rep from * across.

On following rows, knit the purls and purl the knits.

directions

CO 72 (78, 82, 88, 96, 102) sts.

Work 4 rows in seed st. On the last row, place removable stitch markers 4 sts in from each end. Maintain seed st borders outside the markers.

Continue the garment as follows:

Row 1 (RS): Work 4 sts in seed st, slip marker (sm), k to next marker, sm, work 4 sts in seed st.

Row 2 (WS): Work 4 sts in seed st, sm, p to marker, sm, work 4 sts in seed st.

Rep these 2 rows until front measures 12.5 (14, 15.5, 19, 22.5, 24)", ending with a WS row.

SIZE
2 (4, 6, 8, 10, 12)

FINISHED MEASUREMENTS
Width: 18 (19.5, 20.5, 22, 24, 25.5)"

To fit chest circumference: 21 (23, 25, 26.5, 28, 30)"

Length: 16 (18, 20, 24, 28, 30)"

MATERIALS
- Spud & Chloë *Sweater* (55% superwash wool, 45% organic cotton; 160 yd. per 100g skein); color: 7510 Splash, 3 (4, 5, 6, 7, 8) skeins
- US 8 (5mm) circular needle, 24" length (*or size needed to match gauge*)

continued ➤

➤ continued

- extra US 8 (5mm) needle
- 1 (2, 2, 3, 3, 3) button(s) or toggle(s), 1"
- Removable stitch markers
- Stitch holder or scrap yarn
- Tapestry needle

GAUGE

16 sts × 22 rows = 4" in St st, blocked

SKILLS USED

Stockinette stitch, seed stitch, basic increasing and decreasing, simple buttonholes, picking up stitches, three-needle bind-off, backward loop cast-on

divide for placket

When working the first half of the placket, you will also make buttonholes, so please read through this entire section before starting.

Next row (RS): Work 34 (37, 39, 42, 46, 49) sts in established patt. Work next 4 sts in seed st. Place remaining 34 (37, 39, 42, 46, 49) sts on a stitch holder or scrap yarn.

Left Front

Continue on these 38 (41, 43, 46, 50, 53) sts, keeping the seed st borders at both sides until the placket measures 1" ending on a WS row.

Make Buttonhole

Next row (RS): Work in seed st for 4 sts, k to last 4 sts, p1, yo, ssk, k1.

Continue in patt as established, making an additional 0 (1, 1, 2, 2, 2) buttonhole(s) on RS rows at 1" intervals. Work even until placket measures 1.5 (2, 2.5, 3, 3.5, 4)" ending with a RS row.

Next row (WS): Work first 4 (4, 4, 4, 5, 6) sts at placket edge in set patt, then place these sts onto a stitch holder, work in patt to end of row.

Next row (RS): Work in patt.

Next row (WS): BO 2 (2, 2, 3, 3, 3) sts at neck edge, work to end of row.

Continuing in patt, BO 1 st at neck edge on the next 4 (4, 4, 5, 6, 6) WS rows. 28 (31, 33, 34, 36, 38) sts.

Work 5 more rows without shaping, ending with a RS row. Place these 28 (31, 33, 34, 36, 38) sts on another stitch holder and return the 34 (37, 39, 42, 46, 49) sts held for right front to the working needles.

Right Front

With WS facing, pick up and knit 4 sts in the purl bumps just below the seed st placket. Turn work. Work these 4 new sts in seed st starting with a knit st. Work across the rest of the row as est.

Work this side until placket measures 1.5 (2, 2.5, 3, 3.5, 4)" ending with a WS row.

Next row (RS): Work first 4 (4, 4, 4, 5, 6) sts at the placket edge, then transfer them to a stitch holder, work in patt to end of row.

Work 1 row even.

BO 2 (2, 2, 3, 3, 3) sts at neck edge of the next row.

BO 1 st at neck edge on the next 4 (4, 4, 5, 6, 6) RS rows. 28 (31, 33, 34, 36, 38) sts.

Work 4 rows without shaping, ending with a RS row.

back

Next row (WS): Work across the 28 (31, 33, 34, 36, 38) sts in patt, CO 16 (16, 16, 20, 24, 26) sts for back neck using backward loop cast-on, transfer held sts for Left Front to needles and work across them in established patt. 72 (78, 82, 88, 96, 102) sts.

Work all stitches as set—remembering the seed st borders—without shaping until back measures 15 (17, 19, 23, 27, 29)" from CO edge at neck. Work 4 rows across all sts in seed st, then BO all sts.

hood

Transfer sts from stitch holder on the right side of the neck back onto the needle, attach yarn and maintaining 4-st seed st border, work across these sts; pick up and knit 13 (13, 13, 13, 14, 15) sts up the right side of neck; place marker (pm); pick up and knit 16 (16, 16, 20, 24, 26) sts across back of the neck; pm; pick up and knit 13 (13, 13, 13, 14, 15) sts down left side of the neck; work across sts held for left neck, maintaining seed st border.

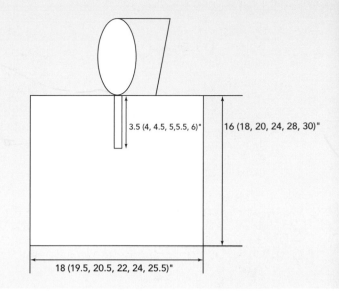

3.5 (4, 4.5, 5, 5.5, 6)"   16 (18, 20, 24, 28, 30)"

18 (19.5, 20.5, 22, 24, 25.5)"

As you work, you will continue the seed st borders at both edges of the hood.

Work 5 (5, 5, 7, 7, 7) rows without shaping.

Inc Row: Work in patt to first marker, sm, m1, work in patt to next marker, m1, sm, work in patt to end.

Rep these 6 (6, 6, 8, 8, 8) rows 9 (10, 11, 11, 12, 12) times.

Work 5 rows without shaping.

Slip half of the sts onto a second needle, and, with WS facing, work the three-needle bind-off.

finishing

Block garment to size shown in the schematic. Sew in all ends and sew on buttons opposite the buttonholes.

FRANCES
retro poncho

by laura nelkin

Little girls *love* wearing ponchos. Designer Laura Nelkin has made them for her daughter ever since she was small. There is something irresistible about being wrapped in a lacy blanket that is designed to stay on your shoulders while you play!

pattern notes

The poncho is composed of two rectangles, each worked from one short side to the other. It features an all-over lace pattern with a three-stitch border on each side. Follow the chart or written directions as indicated for the desired size.

All the charts in this pattern are available for download at **www.wiley.com/go/moreknittinginthesun.**

directions

CO 66 (76, 86) sts, placing markers 3 sts in from each end to mark edging. Beg with Row 1 (a RS row), work the Retro Lace Pattern, following Chart A for sizes 2–4 and 10–12 and Chart B for size 6–8, or follow the written directions if you prefer.

Work the 8 rows of the lace patt 16 (18, 20) times.

BO loosely.

Make a second rectangle the same way.

SIZE
2–4 (6–8, 10–12)

FINISHED MEASUREMENTS
Two pieces, each:
Width: 12.5 (14.5, 16.5)"
Length: 21.5 (24, 26.5)"

MATERIALS
• Schaefer Yarn *Heather* (55% superwash merino wool, 30% cultivated silk, 15% nylon; 400 yd. per 112g skein); color: Apple Green; 1 (2, 2) skein(s)
• US 6 (4mm) needles (*or size needed to match gauge*)
• 2 stitch markers
• 2 removable stitch markers
• Tapestry needle

continued ➤

➤ continued

GAUGE
22 sts × 28 rows = 4" in St st, unblocked

20 sts × 24 rows = 4" in Retro Lace pattern stitch, blocked

SKILLS USED
Lace knitting, whipstitch

Retro Lace Pattern for Sizes 2–4 and 10–12:

Row 1 (RS): K1, yo, k2tog, *k6, k2tog, k2, yo, k1, yo, k2, ssk, k5, rep from * to last 3 sts, k2tog, yo, k1.

Row 2 (WS): K3, *p4, p2tog tbl, p2, yo, p3, yo, p2, p2tog, p5, rep from * to last 3 sts, k3.

Row 3: K1, yo, k2tog, *k4, k2tog, k2, yo, k5, yo, k2, ssk, k3, rep from * to last 3 sts, k2tog, yo, k1.

Row 4: K3, *p2, p2tog tbl, p2, yo, p7, yo, p2, p2tog, p3, rep from * to last 3 sts, k3.

Row 5: K1, yo, k2tog, *k1, yo, k2, ssk, k11, k2tog, k2, yo, rep from * to last 3 sts, k2tog, yo, k1.

Row 6: K3, *p1, yo, p2, p2tog, p9, p2tog tbl, p2, yo, p2, rep from * to last 3 sts, k3.

Row 7: K1, yo, k2tog, *k3, yo, k2, ssk, k7, k2tog, k2, yo, k2, rep from * to last 3 sts, k2tog, yo, k1.

Row 8: K3, *p3, yo, p2, p2tog, p5, p2tog tbl, p2, yo, p4, rep from * to last 3 sts, k3.

Retro Lace Pattern for Size 6–8:

Row 1 (RS): K1, yo, k2tog, *k6, k2tog, k2, yo, k1, yo, k2, ssk, k5, rep from * to last 13 sts, k6, k2tog, k2, yo, k2tog, yo, k1.

Row 2 (WS): K3, p1, yo, p2, p2tog, p5, *p4, p2tog tbl, p2, yo, p3, yo, p2, p2tog, p5, rep from * to last 3 sts, k3.

Row 3: K1, yo, k2tog, *k4, k2tog, k2, yo, k5, yo, k2, ssk, k3, rep from * to last 13 sts, k4, k2tog, k2, yo, k2, k2tog, yo, k1.

Row 4: K3, p3, yo, p2, p2tog, p3, *p2, p2tog tbl, p2, yo, p7, yo, p2, p2tog, p3, rep from * to last 3 sts, k3.

Row 5: K1, yo, k2tog, *k1, yo, k2, ssk, k11, k2tog, k2, yo, rep from * to last 13 sts, k1, yo, k2, ssk, k5, k2tog, yo, k1.

Row 6: K3, p4, p2tog tbl, p2, yo, p2, *p1, yo, p2, p2tog, p9, p2tog tbl, p2, yo, p2, rep from * to last 3 sts, k3.

Row 7: K1, yo, k2tog, *k3, yo, k2, ssk, k7, k2tog, k2, yo, k2, rep from * to last 13 sts, k3, yo, k2, ssk, k3, k2tog, yo, k1.

Row 8: K3, p2, p2tog tbl, p2, yo, p4, *p3, yo, p2, p2tog, p5, p2tog tbl, p2, yo, p4, rep from * to last 3 sts, k3.

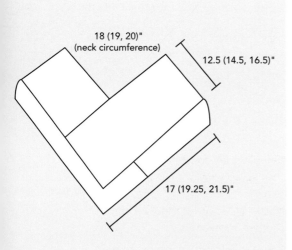

18 (19, 20)"
(neck circumference)

12.5 (14.5, 16.5)"

17 (19.25, 21.5)"

Chart A, Retro Lace Pattern for Sizes 2–4 and 10–12

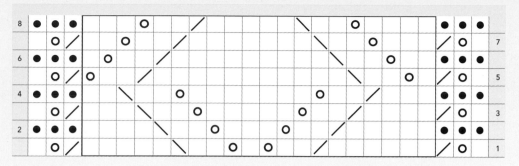

Chart B, Retro Lace Pattern for Sizes 6–8

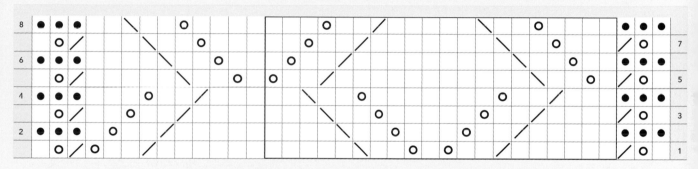

Key to Retro Lace Pattern Charts

☐	**knit** RS: knit WS: purl	
◉	**yo** RS: yarn over WS: yarn over	
◹	**k2tog** RS: k2tog WS: p2tog	
◳	**ssk** RS: ssk WS: p2tog tbl	
▣	**purl** RS: purl WS: knit	

finishing

Weave in ends and wet block to size.

Lay out rectangles with RS facing and place a removable marker 14 (16, 18)" up from bottom on both LH long edges.

Then, with WS facing, lay short end of one rectangle so it lines up with bottom edge and removable marker on long side of other rectangle. Whipstitch in place (see the "Special Knitting Techniques" appendix).

Flip over and repeat with second short side.

OWEN
beach towel blanket

OWEN
beach towel blanket

by kristi porter

When my daughter was small, she used an orange beach towel as her blankie. It seemed like a strange choice at first, but the size was just right to wrap up in and fit well on her child-size bed, plus it was sturdy and machine washable. So, I incorporated the bold stripes and proportions of the quintessential beach towel for this kid's blanket.

Since the knitting is so easy, this is a great project for a child to practice a few stitches on here and there. Once he or she gets the hang of it, maybe your child will even want to create a coordinating pillow with the leftover yarn. Organized or random stripes will both work well!

directions

With Color A, CO 150 sts.

Knit 36 rows (18 garter ridges will be visible).

Switch to Color D and knit 2 rows.

Switch to Color B and knit 36 rows.

Switch to Color D and knit 2 rows.

Switch to Color C and knit 36 rows.

Switch to Color D and knit 2 rows.

Switch to Color B and knit 36 rows.

Switch to Color D and knit 2 rows.

Switch to Color A and knit 36 rows.

BO loosely (use a larger needle, if necessary).

finishing

Weave in ends.

FINISHED MEASUREMENTS
Width: 30"
Length: 54"

MATERIALS
- Berroco *Comfort Chunky* (50% superfine nylon, 50% superfine acrylic; 150 yd. per 100g skein); [A] color: 5753 Aegean Sea, 3 skeins; [B] color: 5721 Sprig, 3 skeins; [C] color: 5720 Hummus, 2 skeins; [D] color: 5745 Filbert, 1 skein
- US 13 (9mm) circular needle, 36" length or longer (*or size needed to match gauge*)
- Tapestry needle

GAUGE
12 sts × 24 rows = 4" in garter stitch, unblocked

SKILLS USED
Knit stitch, changing colors

HUCK
fishing hat

by kristi porter

his hat surely belongs in the summer wardrobe of every youngster! With the styling of a classic fisherman's hat, it's appropriate for boys and girls and the wide brim keeps the sun off delicate faces. The millinery wire is optional, but does provide some added structure to the brim.

pattern notes

This pattern uses millinery wire to support the broad brim of the hat. You can find it online and in some craft stores. You can also substitute any other sturdy, rustproof wire.

For instructions on provisional cast-on and grafting, please refer to the "Special Knitting Techniques" appendix.

three-needle join

To create the welt detailing on this hat you use a three-needle join as follows: You will have two equal sets of stitches, six rows apart, on two circular needles. With RS facing, bring the lower needle up and hold it parallel and behind the working needle in the left hand. *Insert the RH working needle into the first stitch on the front needle and then into the first stitch on the back needle; knit these 2 sts together. Rep from * around. You will end up with the original number of sts on the working needle.

directions

Using the 16" circular needle and a provisional cast-on and scrap yarn, CO 144 (162, 180) sts.

Switch to main yarn, join in the round, and knit 6 rows.

SIZE
2–4 (6–8, 10–12)

FINISHED MEASUREMENTS
Head circumference: 16 (18, 20)"

MATERIALS
- Zitron *Polo* (60% cotton, 40% acrylic; 153 yd. per 50g ball); color: 110 Beige; 1 (2, 2) skein(s)
- US 5 (3.75mm) circular needle, 16" length *(or size needed to match gauge)*
- US 5 (3.75mm) circular needle, 24" length or longer
- US 5 (3.75mm) double-pointed needles
- 1 yd. millinery wire *(optional)*

continued ▶

➤ continued

- Scrap yarn
- Stitch markers

GAUGE
24 sts × 32 rows = 4" in St st

SKILLS USED
Knitting in the round, provisional cast-on, three-needle join, grafting

Unravel the provisional cast-on and transfer these live sts to the spare needle. Join the two sets of sts using the three-needle join.

NOTE If you plan to insert millinery wire later, leave the last 5 sts from the provisional cast-on on scrap yarn and knit the last 5 sts from only the working needle. This will leave an opening to insert the wire.

shape brim

Set-up Round: *K18, place marker (pm), rep from * around.

Next round: *K to 2 sts before marker, k2tog, slip marker (sm), rep from * around. 8 (9, 10) sts dec'd.

Next round: Knit.

Rep these 2 rounds 5 more times. 96 (108, 120) sts.

If desired, you can remove the markers now and replace them, at 12-st intervals, when you begin shaping the crown.

create welt

Run the spare needle through all the sts on the needle, so both needles are in the sts. Knit 6 rows with the working needle, leaving the spare needle in place. *(It will be awkward to knit at first: persevere.)* Join sts on both needles using the three-needle join.

Knit even for an additional 2 (2.5, 3)".

Rep the steps above to create another welt.

shape crown

Switch to dpns when necessary as you decrease.

Next round: *K to 2 sts before marker, k2tog, sm, rep from * around. 8 (9, 10) sts dec'd.

Next round: Knit.

Rep these 2 rounds 10 more times. 8 (9, 10) sts.

Cut yarn and thread tail through rem sts. Secure the end on the WS of hat and weave in end.

finishing

If desired, wet block the hat. A plastic food storage container or cereal bowl (open side up) makes a good hat form.

If you are using the millinery wire, cut a length a couple of inches longer than the circumference of the edge of the brim. Using the opening, thread the wire into the welt at the outside edge of the brim. When the hat has the desired shape, cut the ends of the wire so they overlap slightly and tape them together with a small piece of duct tape. Remove the remaining length of scrap yarn and graft these live sts to the corresponding sts 6 rows below. Weave in ends.

ELOISE
mini cloche

by anne kuo lukito

This cloche is simple, yet versatile. Shaping at the brim gives it a slight bell shape. A child can wear the brim down or folded up with any of the accessories to suit your kid's mood or outfit.

directions

Divide yarn into two balls. With yarn held double and circular needle, CO 78 (84, 90) sts. Join for working in the round, being careful not to twist sts.

Round 1: Purl.

Round 2: Knit.

Rep last 2 rounds 1 (2, 2) more time(s).

Knit 3 (4, 4) rounds.

Next round: *K24 (26, 28), k2tog, rep from * to end of round.

Knit 3 (4, 4) rounds.

Next round: *K23 (25, 27), k2tog, rep from * to end of round. 72 (78, 84) sts.

Work in St st until work measures 4.5 (5, 5.5)" from CO edge.

shape crown

Switch to dpns when necessary as you decrease for the crown.

Set-up Round: *K12 (13, 14), place marker (pm), rep from * to end of round.

Dec Round: *K to 2 sts before marker, k2tog, slip marker (sm), rep from * to end of round. 6 sts dec'd.

Next round: Knit.

Rep the last 2 rounds until 12 sts rem.

SIZE
2–4 (6–8, 10–12)

FINISHED MEASUREMENTS
Brim circumference: 17.75 (19.25, 20.5)"

Head circumference: 16.5 (17.75, 19.25)"

MATERIALS
- Louet *Euroflax Sport Weight* (100% wet spun linen; 270 yd. per 100g skein); Color: 55 Willow, 1 (1, 1) skein
- 30–50 yd. in a contrasting or coordinating color of the same yarn for each accessory

continued ➤

➤ continued

- US 7 (4.5mm) circular needle, 16" length *(or size needed to match gauge)*
- US 7 (4.5mm) double-pointed needles
- US 6 (4mm) needles *(for accessories only)*
- 6 stitch markers
- Stitch holder or scrap yarn
- Tapestry needle
- 1 pin back for each accessory *(available at most craft stores)*
- Sewing needle and coordinating thread

GAUGE

17.5 sts × 23 rows = 4" in St st with yarn held double and blocked

SKILLS USED

Working in the round, backward loop cast-on, working on dpns, basic shaping, sewing (for attaching pin-back to accessories)

Next round: K2tog around.

Cut yarn, leaving a 6" tail. Draw tail through rem loops and secure.

accessories

Bow

Using smaller needles and contrasting yarn held doubled, CO 17 sts.

Row 1: Sl 1, [k1, p1] to end of row.

Row 2: Sl 1, [p1, k1] to end of row.

Rep Rows 1 and 2 until work measures 4", or desired length from CO edge.

Hold piece so that the ribbing runs horizontally, pinch and gather the rectangle at the center. Wrap a length of yarn several times around and secure. Block bow. With sewing needle and coordinating thread, sew pin back to WS of bow. Steam the bow or re-block as necessary.

Flower

Using smaller needles and contrasting yarn held doubled, CO 3 sts.

Row 1 (WS): [Kfb] twice, k1. 5 sts.

Row 2 (RS): Kfb, k2, kfb, k1. 7 sts.

Rows 3, 5, 7, 8, 9, 11, and 13: Knit.

Row 4: Kfb, k to last 2 sts, kfb, k1. 9 sts.

Row 6: Rep Row 4. 11 sts.

Row 10: K2tog, k to last 2 sts, ssk. 9 sts.

Row 12: [K2tog] twice, k to last 4 sts, [ssk] twice. 5 sts.

Cut yarn and place sts on stitch holder. Make 3 more petals, or as many as desired. Using tapestry needle, thread yarn through the held sts of all the petals, then join them together in a circle, drawing tight.

Weave in ends and block. With sewing needle and coordinating thread, sew pin back to WS of flower. Steam the flower or re-block as necessary.

Rosette

Using smaller needles and contrasting yarn held doubled, CO 20 sts using the backward loop cast-on (see the "Special Knitting Techniques" appendix).

Row 1 (RS): Knit.

Row 2 (WS): Purl, CO 8 sts. 28 sts.

Row 3: [K8, k2tog] twice, k8. 26 sts.

Row 4: Rep Row 2. 34 sts.

Row 5: K8, [k2tog, k4] to last 2 sts, k2. 30 sts.

Rows 6 and 8: Purl.

Row 7: [K2tog, k4] to end. 25 sts.

Row 9: [K2tog, k3] to end. 20 sts.

BO all sts.

Block strip. With strip flat and WS up, roll the strip starting with the wider end and gently gathering the bound-off edge to form the base of the rosette. Using coordinating thread, tack the base of the rosette together so that it does not unroll. Then sew the pin back to the underside of the rosette. Steam the rosette or re-block as necessary.

finishing

Weave in ends and block.

Attach desired accessory!

CADDIE
summer carry-all

CADDIE

summer carry-all

by kristi porter

This drawstring backpack with a simple all-over pattern holds all of summer's necessities and is easy for a child to carry when he or she needs a hands-free way to run or ride or climb. Creating the multi-colored drawstrings is a great way to introduce a child to working with yarn, whether they are made with a knitting spool, finger knitting, or a simple finger crochet chain.

pattern notes

Sl 5: Slip 5 sts purlwise to the RH needle without knitting them.

For provisional cast-on, grafting, I-cord, and three-needle bind-off instructions, please refer to the "Special Knitting Techniques" appendix.

directions

This bag is worked in the round from bottom to top.

Using a provisional cast-on and scrap yarn, CO 120 sts.

Switch to MC yarn, knit 1 round and join, being careful not to twist sts.

FINISHED MEASUREMENTS
12" wide × 14" long

MATERIALS

- Zitron *Polo* (60% cotton, 40% acrylic; 153 yd. per 50g ball); [MC] color: 112 light grey, 3 balls; [CC] color: 635 multicolored, 1 ball

- US 6 (4mm) circular needle, 24" length *(or size needed to match gauge)*

- US 6 (4mm) double-pointed needles (for drawstrings)

continued ➤

➤ continued

- Spare US 6 (4mm) circular needle, 24" length
- Scrap yarn
- Tapestry needle
- Safety pin

GAUGE

20 sts × 40 rows = 4" over Bow-Tie Pattern, unblocked

SKILLS USED

Knitting in the round, provisional cast-on, grafting, I-cord, three-needle bind-off

Begin Bow-Tie Pattern as follows:

Round 1: *K5, bring yarn to front, sl 5, bring yarn to back, rep from * around.

Round 2: Knit.

Rep these 2 rounds 3 more times, then Round 1 once more. There are 5 floats in each set.

Round 10: *K7, insert RH needle under the 5 floats from bottom to top and k the next st, bring the 5 floats up and over the needle and the st just worked, k2, rep from * around.

Round 11: *Bring yarn to front, sl 5, bring yarn to back, k5, rep from * around.

Round 12: Knit.

Rep these 2 rounds 3 more times, then Round 11 once more.

Round 20: *K2, insert RH needle under the 5 floats from bottom to top and k the next st, bring the 5 floats up and over the needle and the st just worked, k7, rep from * around.

Rep these 20 rounds 6 more times, or until bag measures 1" less than desired length, ending with Round 10 or Round 20.

create drawstring casing

Next round: Purl.

**Row 1 (RS): K1, p1, k56, p1, k1; turn. You will now work back and forth on these 60 sts only.

Row 2 (WS): P1, k1, p to last 2 sts, k1, p1.

Rep these 2 rows twice more.

Purl 1 RS row to create turning ridge.

Work 6 more rows as above, beginning with a WS row.

Fold casing to WS at turning ridge, cut yarn, and graft live sts to the backs of sts from the first round of casing.**

Join yarn to remaining 60 sts with RS facing and work ** to ** to complete the second half of casing.

finishing

drawstrings

Using CC and dpns, CO 4 sts. Make an I-cord 48" long. Make a second drawstring the same way. The drawstrings can also be made with a knitting spool, finger knitting, or finger crochet, if preferred. The drawstrings shown in the photos were made by my daughter with a knitting spool.

Lay the bag flat with the openings of the casings at the sides and the provisional cast-on nearest you. With a tapestry needle, secure one end of one drawstring to the bottom right corner of the bag, just above the provisional cast-on. Attach a safety pin to the opposite end of the drawstring and feed it through the back casing from right to left, then through the top casing from left to right. Bring the end back down to the bottom of the bag and secure it just above the opposite end of the drawstring. Attach the second drawstring the same way to the bottom left corner, and feed it through the back casing from left to right, then through the front casing from right to left. Secure the end to the bottom left corner of the bag.

join bottom of bag

Remove provisional cast-on and transfer 60 live sts each to two needles, being sure that stitches are divided at the same points as the top of the bag. Turn the work inside out. Join the bottom of the bag by working a three-needle bind-off.

Weave in ends, being sure that drawstrings are firmly attached.

BOTTOMS

MILO
cargo shorts

MILO
cargo shorts
by carol feller

Little children love to run, jump, and be active. The loose, comfortable fit of these shorts allows kids to climb rocks and still look smart enough to take out to dinner! Knit entirely in the round from the top down, these shorts are easy to try on your little one as your knitting progresses to ensure the perfect fit.

pattern notes

For RLI and LLI increases, I-cord bind-off, grafting, whipstitch, picking up stitches, and specific cast ons used in this pattern, please refer to the "Special Knitting Techniques" appendix.

directions
waistband

With dpns, CO 3 sts and create an I-cord 12" long. BO.

With scrap yarn and provisional cast-on, CO 132 (136, 142, 148, 154, 160) sts to longer circular needle. With working yarn, join to work in the round, place marker (pm) for start of round, and knit 11 rounds.

Purl 1 round to create turning ridge.

Knit 5 rounds.

Eyelet Round: K60 (62, 65, 68, 71, 74), *k2tog, yo2, ssk*, k4, rep from * to * once, k to end of round.

SIZE
2 (4, 6, 8, 10, 12)

FINISHED MEASUREMENTS
Waist circumference: 22 (22.5, 23.5, 24.5, 25.5, 26.5)"
Length: 14.5 (16.5, 18.5, 21, 23, 25)"

MATERIALS
- Louet *MerLin Sport Weight* (60% wet spun linen, 40% merino; 250 yd. per 100g skein); color: 43 Pewter; 2 (3, 3, 3, 4, 4) skeins
- US 3 (3.25mm) circular needle, 24" length—shorter length may be needed for smaller sizes (*or size needed to match gauge*)
- US 3 (3.25mm) circular needle, 16" length

continued ➤

➤ continued

- US 3 (3.25mm) double-pointed needles
- Size D (3.25mm) crochet hook
- 0.5"-wide elastic, 21 (21.5, 22.5, 23.5, 24.5, 25.5)" length
- Tapestry needle
- Scrap yarn
- 2 stitch markers
- 4 split-ring stitch markers

GAUGE

24 sts × 32 rows = 4" in St st, blocked

SKILLS USED

Increases, picking up stitches, knitting in the round, working on dpns, I-cord, grafting, provisional cast-on, backward loop cast-on, cable cast-on, whipstitch

22 (22.5, 23.5, 24.5, 25.5, 26.5)"

7.5 (8.5, 9, 10, 11, 11.5)"

7 (8, 9.5, 11, 12, 13.5)"

16 (17, 18, 19.5, 21, 23.5)"

Knit 5 rounds, working 2 sts into the yo2's in the previous round.

Pull I-cord through eyelets at front and knot each end to ensure it stays in place.

Cut elastic to desired length (suggested lengths given in "Materials" list), overlap by approx 0.5", and sew securely together. This will ensure that the elastic is slightly smaller than waist for snug fit. Position this elastic in waistband casing when joining round is being worked.

Joining Round: Undo provisional cast-on, placing sts on shorter circular needle. Fold at purled turning ridge, and with second needle behind and working needle in front, *knit first st from each needle tog; rep from * until all sts have been worked and waistband is joined. Note that elastic is now inside waistband.

Knit 1 round.

hip shaping

Set-up Round: Start of round marker indicates center back. K66 (68, 71, 74, 77, 80), pm for center front, k to end of round. Place 4 dart markers (split-ring) 16 (17, 18, 18, 19, 20) sts before and after front and back markers.

Next round (Hip Inc Round): *K to dart m, slip marker (sm), LLI, k to next dart m, RLI, sm; rep from *, k to end of round. 4 sts inc'd.

Rep Hip Inc Round every 5 (4, 3, 2, 2, 2) rounds 1 (1, 3, 2, 1, 7) time(s) and then every 0 (5, 0, 3, 3, 3) rounds 0 (1, 0, 3, 5, 1) time(s). 140 (148, 158, 172, 182, 196) sts.

Remove dart markers.

Work even until piece measures approx 3 (3.5, 3.5, 4, 4.5, 4.5)".

crotch shaping

Next round (Crotch Inc Round): *K to m (seam st), work RLI tbl, sm, k tbl (seam st), LLI tbl, rep from *, k to end. 4 sts inc'd.

Rep Crotch Inc Round every 6 (6, 6, 6, 6, 5) rounds 5 (4, 7, 7, 6, 7) times, then every 5 (5, 0, 5, 5, 4) rounds 1 (3, 0, 1, 3, 5) time(s). 168 (180, 190, 208, 222, 248) sts.

Work should now measure approx 7.5 (8.5, 9, 10, 11, 11.5)".

right leg

With shorter circular needle, knit to front m; leave rem 84 (90, 95, 104, 111, 124) sts held on longer circular needle for second leg.

Using backward loop cast-on method, CO 12 (12, 13, 14, 15, 16) sts. Pm at center of these newly CO sts for new start of round. 96 (102, 108, 118, 126, 140) sts.

Using shorter circular needle, join to work in the round.

**Work even in St st until leg measures 7 (8, 9.5, 11, 12, 13.5)" from CO sts or to 1–2" below child's knee.

Purl 1 round to create turning ridge.

Knit 9 rounds.

Break yarn leaving long tail.

Fold at purled turning ridge. With tapestry needle, whipstitch live sts to WS of leg.**

left leg

With shorter circular needle, starting at center of CO sts on first leg, pick up and knit 6 (6, 6, 7, 7, 8) sts, knit held sts, pick up and knit rem 6 (6, 7, 7, 8, 8) sts from CO sts on first leg, pm for start of round. 96 (102, 108, 118, 126, 140) sts.

Work as for first leg from ** to **.

pockets

With shorter circular needle, CO 42 (50, 52, 60, 68, 70) sts.

Next row (RS): K17 (20, 21, 24, 27, 28), sl 1, k6 (8, 8, 10, 12, 12), sl 1, k to end of row.

Next row (WS): Purl.

Rep these 2 rows until pocket measures 5 (5.5, 6, 6.5, 7, 7.5)" ending with a WS row.

Pleat Row (RS): K9 (10, 11, 12, 13, 14).

Make first pleat as follows: Sl 4 (5, 5, 6, 7, 7) sts to first dpn, sl 4 (5, 5, 6, 7, 7) sts to second dpn, fold work so that the second dpn is **behind** the first dpn and parallel with WS touching; 4 (5, 5, 6, 7, 7) sts from LH working needle are behind the 2 dpns. Insert working needle into first st on first dpn, first st from second dpn, and first st from LH needle; k these 3 sts tog; rep until all 4 (5, 5, 6, 7, 7) sts are joined.

Make second pleat as follows: Sl 4 (5, 5, 6, 7, 7) sts to first dpn, sl 4 (5, 5, 6, 7, 7) sts to second dpn, and fold work so that the second dpn is in **front** of the first with RS touching; 4 (5, 5, 6, 7, 7) sts from the LH working needle are in front of the 2 dpns. Insert working needle through first st on LH needle, second dpn, then first dpn and k these 3 sts tog; rep until all 4 (5, 5, 6, 7, 7) sts are joined, k to end of row.

Work 1 more WS row.

BO all sts using I-cord bind-off.

Rep for second pocket.

finishing

Fold pockets along pleat lines, and tack along the bottom edge to keep the pleats in place. Sew pockets in place at sides of legs.

Weave in loose ends using tapestry needle. Block to dimensions given on schematic.

KIMO
board shorts

KIMO
board shorts

by kendra nitta

These supersoft board shorts are perfect for lounging around poolside and can even double as pajama bottoms! The asymmetrical stripes provide endless possibilities to mix and match colors to suit boys or girls. Working seamlessly from the top down makes it easy to customize the length for your child. Short rows, double knitting, and stripes add just the right amount of challenge for newer knitters ready to take their skills to the next level. *Note: These shorts are not intended as swimwear.*

pattern notes

The casing and lower part of the waistband are worked in double knitting, so that the stitches for both the right side and the wrong side of the waistband are on the needle at the same time. You'll use two different balls of yarn: Ball 1 is the yarn that you used for the original cast on, and Ball 2 is the second ball that you join when you start the double knitting section.

The pattern is written for an elastic waistband with a decorative-only front tie. Instructions are also provided for a working I-cord drawstring that can be used with or without the grommets.

Directions for an optional patch pocket (not shown) in contrasting color are given.

For M1L and M1R increases, cast-on techniques, and I-cord instructions, please refer to the "Special Knitting Techniques" appendix.

SIZE
2 (4, 6)

FINISHED MEASUREMENTS
Waist circumference (before inserting elastic or drawstring): 24 (25.5, 27)"
Length (measured from center front to bottom of inseam): 10.5 (12, 13)"

MATERIALS
- Knit Picks *Shine Worsted* (60% pima cotton, 40% Modal®; 75 yd. per 50g ball); [MC] 2 (2, 3) balls; [CC1] 2 (2, 3) balls; [CC2] 1 (1, 2) ball(s)
- Larger sample shown uses [MC] 23805 Bachelor Button, [CC1] 23799 Cream, and [CC2] 23801 Grass
- Smaller sample shown uses [MC] 23801 Grass, [CC1] 23799 Cream, and [CC2] 23797 Crocus
- 2 US 7 (4.5mm) circular needles, 24" length *(or size needed to match gauge)*
- US 7 (4.5mm) circular needle, 16" length

continued ➤

➤ continued

- Stitch markers, 1 locking
- Scrap yarn
- Cable needle
- 0.5" grommets, 2 sets (optional)
- 0.5" waistband elastic, 1 package (optional)
- Tapestry needle
- Sewing needle and thread (if using elastic)
- Safety pin

GAUGE

18 sts × 28 rows = 4" in St st, unblocked

Note: You can use the pocket as your gauge swatch.

SKILLS USED

Double knitting, short rows, stripes, I-cord, provisional cast-on

directions
waistband

Using one longer circular needle and CC1, CO 108 (116, 124) sts using provisional cast-on. Place marker (pm) and join for working in the round, taking care not to twist sts. Knit 4 (4, 5) rounds.

Turning Round: *K2, yo, rep from * to end of round.

Next round: K all sts, dropping yo's without working them.

Knit 4 (5, 5) rounds.

Carefully undo provisional cast-on and place resulting 108 (116, 124) sts on second longer circular needle. *NOTE: If you find you only have 107 (115, 123) sts from the provisional cast-on, CO 1 st using the backward loop method at the end of the next round.* Holding sts from provisional cast-on behind working needle, *K1 from front needle, k1 from back needle, rep from * to end of round. 216 (232, 248) sts.

Use locking stitch marker to mark RS of piece.

Double-knit Casing
Join Ball 2 of CC1 and begin double-knit casing. Slip all sts purlwise.

Round 1: Using only Ball 1,*k1, sl1 wyif, rep from * to end of round, leaving working yarn in front.

Round 2: With RS still facing, using only Ball 2: *Sl 1 wyib, p1, rep from * to end of round, leaving working yarn in back.

Rep these 2 rounds once more.

Work Eyelets
Next round: With Ball 1, [K1, sl 1 wyif] 78 (84, 90) times, sl 1 to CN and hold in front, yo (taking care to bring yarn to front again), sl 1 wyif, return st from CN to LH needle and ssk, [sl 1 wyif, k1] twice, sl 1 wyif, sl 1 wyib, sl 1 to CN and hold in back, return st from RH needle to LH needle and k2tog, sl 1 from CN wyif, yo (taking care to bring yarn to front again), sl 1 wyif, *k1, sl 1 wyif, rep from * to end of round.

Rep Round 2 (under "Double-knit Casing") once, then work Rounds 1 and 2 once more.

Next round: Using Ball 2, k every st to close casing.

Double-knit Waistband

Round 1: Using only Ball 1, *p1, sl 1 wyib, rep from * to end of round, leaving working yarn in back.

Round 2: With RS still facing, using only Ball 2: *Sl 1 wyif, k1, rep from * to end of round, leaving working yarn in front.

Rep these 2 rounds 5 (6, 8) times more.

Break yarn. Piece measures approximately 2.5 (2.75, 3)" from CO edge.

body

Join MC, *k2tog, rep from * to end of round. 108 (116, 124) sts.

Move end of round marker 1 st to the right. Work 1 round even.

Join CC2, knit 1 round.

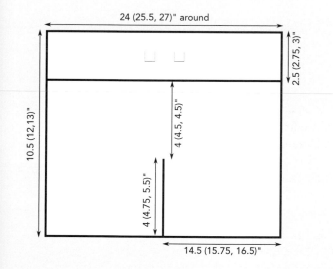

24 (25.5, 27)" around

2.5 (2.75, 3)"

10.5 (12,13)"

4 (4.5, 4.5)"

4 (4.75, 5.5)"

14.5 (15.75, 16.5)"

left side

Short rows are used to shape the hips and rear. When you encounter a wrapped stitch on subsequent rows, work the wrap together with the stitch it wraps. (See the "Special Knitting Techniques" appendix for details on how to work short rows, including wrap & turn [w&t].)

Row 1 (RS): K2 (2, 2), w&t.

Row 2: P4 (4, 4), w&t.

Row 3: K6 (6, 6), w&t.

Row 4: P8 (8, 8), w&t.

Row 5: K12 (11, 11), w&t.

Row 6: P16 (14, 14), w&t.

Row 7: K21 (17, 18), w&t.

Row 8: P26 (20, 22), w&t.

Size 2 only: Continue with Right Side instructions.

Row 9: K – (25, 28), w&t.

Row 10: P – (30, 34), w&t.

right side

Work across to right side and begin shaping as follows:

Next row: K69 (75, 81), w&t.

Work Rows 2–8 (2–10, 2–10) from Left Side instructions (above).

K to marker. Work 0 (1, 1) more round(s) with CC2. Break CC2.

Change to MC.

Row 1 (RS): K30 (34, 36), w&t.

Row 2: P6 (6, 6), w&t.

Row 3: K9 (9, 9), w&t.

Row 4: P12 (12, 12), w&t.

Row 5: K15 (15, 15), w&t.

Row 6: P18 (18, 18), w&t.

Row 7: K21 (21, 21), w&t.

Row 8: P24 (24, 24), w&t.

Row 9: K27 (27, 27), w&t.

Row 10: P30 (30, 30), w&t.

Row 11: K33 (33, 33), w&t.

Row 12: P36 (36, 36), w&t.

Row 13: K39 (38, 38), w&t.

Row 14: P42 (40, 40), w&t.

Row 15: K45 (42, 42), w&t.

Row 16: P48 (44, 44), w&t.

Row 17: K50 (46, 46), w&t.

Row 18: P52 (48, 48), w&t.

Size 2 only: Continue with Row 1 of Front Short Rows (below).

Row 19: K – (50, 50), w&t.

Row 20: P – (52, 52), w&t.

Row 21: K – (54, 54), w&t.

Row 22: P – (56, 56), w&t.

Size 4 only: Continue with Row 1 of Front Short Rows (below).

Row 23: K – (–, 58), w&t.

Row 24: P – (–, 60), w&t.

Front Short Rows

Row 1: K93 (101, 109), w&t.

Row 2 (WS): P26 (30, 34), w&t.

Row 3: K31 (35, 39), w&t.

Row 4: P36 (40, 44), w&t.

Row 5: K41 (43, 48) w&t.

Row 6: P46 (46, 52), w&t.

Row 7: K – (49, 55), w&t.

Row 8: P – (52, 58), w&t.

K to marker. Work even in MC until there are 22 (24, 25) rounds from front center waistband, not counting waistband rounds.

increase for legs

You will now increase on each side of the center "seam" on the front and back of the shorts.

Set-up Round: K25 (27, 29), M1R, k2, place marker (pm), k2, M1L, k52 (56, 60), pm, k to end of round. 110 (118, 126) sts.

Work 1 round even.

Inc Round: K to 2 sts before Back marker, M1R, k4, M1L, k to 2 sts before front marker, M1R, k4, M1L, k to end of round. 114 (122, 130) sts.

Work 1 round even.

TIP Run a length of smooth scrap yarn through this round of sts and your child will be able to try on the shorts. Work additional even rounds if you want to lengthen the rise of the shorts before dividing for the legs.

Rep Inc Round once more. 118 (126, 134) sts.

divide for legs

K29 (31, 33) sts, sl 1. Place next 59 (63, 67) sts for Right Leg on scrap yarn. Transfer rem 59 (63, 67) sts for Left Leg to 16" needle, removing end-of-round marker. Break yarn.

Make Crotch Gusset

Using scrap yarn, provisionally cast on 12 (14, 14) sts to one of the longer circular needles for the crotch. Purl across these sts with MC. Pick up the 16" needle holding the sts for the left leg, holding it so the slipped st is at the tip of the RH needle. Transfer the 12 (14, 14) newly cast-on sts to the LH needle with the working yarn to the right. Slip the first st on the RH needle (the previously slipped st) to LH needle, ssk, k5 (6, 6), pm to indicate beg of round.

Round 1: K5 (6, 6), k2tog, k to end of round. 69 (75, 79) sts.

Round 2: Change to CC2, k to last 6 (7, 7) sts, ssk, k to end of round. 68 (74, 78) sts.

Round 3: K4 (5, 5), k2tog, k to end of round. 67 (73, 77) sts.

Round 4: K to last 5 (6, 6) sts, ssk, k to end of round. 66 (72, 76) sts.

Round 5: K3 (4, 4), k2tog, k to end of round. 65 (71, 75) sts.

left leg

Work in CC2 until the leg stripe is 12 (14, 17) rounds total.

Work 2 (3, 4) rounds MC.

Work 4 (5, 6) rounds CC1.

Work 4 (5, 6) rounds MC.

Check length, and work additional MC rounds if desired, stopping 0.5" before desired length.

Change to CC2 and knit 1 round, then purl 3 rounds.

BO loosely in purl.

right leg

Transfer Right Leg sts from scrap yarn to 16" needle. Carefully remove scrap yarn from the 12 (14, 14) sts provisionally cast on for crotch and place these sts on LH needle.

Work crotch gusset as for Left Leg, using MC throughout.

Work 3 (3, 5) more rounds in MC.

Change to CC2 and work 10 (12, 14) rounds.

Change to MC and work 6 (9, 11) rounds.

Change to CC2 and k 1 round, then p 3 rounds.

BO loosely in purl.

drawstring

If using grommets, install in waistband eyelets according to package directions.

NOTE Practice installing grommets *before* installing them on the finished piece.

Using CC1, make a 3-st I-cord. Work for 22" for decorative tie or 40 (41, 42)" for a functioning drawstring. BO.

pocket

Using 16" circular needle and CC1, CO 17 (19, 21) sts.

Beg with a purl row, work in St st for 4 rows.

Turning Row (WS): *P2, yo, rep from * to last 3 sts, p3.

Next row: Knit, dropping all yos without working them.

Work in St st for 3 more rows.

Row 1 (RS): K16 (18, 20), sl 1, CO 2 sts using backward loop method.

Row 2: P19 (21, 23), CO 2 sts using backward loop method.

Row 3: K2, sl 1, k to last 3 sts, sl 1, k2.

Row 4: Purl.

Cont working Rows 3 and 4 until pocket measures 3.25 (3.5, 3.75)" from CO, ending with a knit row.

Row 1 (WS): P2, k17 (19, 21), p2.

Row 2: K2, sl 1 wyib, p to last 3 sts, sl 1 wyib, k2.

Row 3: BO 2, k to last 2 sts, p2.

Row 4: BO 2, p to end.

Row 5: BO.

finishing

Cut elastic to 21.5 (22, 23)" or child's waist measurement. Insert elastic into casing using safety pin small enough to fit through eyelets. Overlap ends by 0.5" and sew together using needle and thread. Using safety pin, insert I-cord through eyelets.

Carefully sew down pocket to right hip.

Machine wash, block lightly.

OLIVIA
bubble skirt

OLIVIA
bubble skirt
by beautia dew

L ittle girls and big girls alike will love this fun and flouncy bubble skirt. It's perfect on its own, but pairs well with tights or leggings in cooler weather. The skirt is knit in stockinette stitch in the round from the waist down. Increasing and decreasing create the ruched ruffles.

pattern notes

Make sure to weave in loose ends as you go since creating the ruffles hides the wrong side of the work.

directions

Cut elastic 20 (21, 22, 23, 23.5)" long. Overlap 0.5" and sew.

Using smaller needles, CO 108 (112, 118, 122, 126) sts. Place marker (pm) and join for knitting in the round.

Work in St st for 4 rounds or length needed to cover elastic.

Next round: Purl to create hem fold.

Work in St st for 4 rounds.

Next round: Place elastic against WS of work. Fold work over elastic so the CO edge and sts on needle can be knit together. Knit together each st on LH needle with a CO edge st to encase elastic.

Sizes 4, 6, and 12:

Next round: [K27 (28, 21), pm] 4 (4, 6) times.

Sizes 8 and 10:

Next round: [K24, pm, k23 (25), pm] twice, k24, pm.

Knit 4 rounds.

SIZE
4 (6, 8, 10, 12)

FINISHED MEASUREMENTS
Waist circumference: 21.5 (22.5, 23.5, 24.5, 25)", before adding elastic
Length: 11 (12, 13.5, 15, 16)"

MATERIALS
- Classic Elite Yarns *Provence* (100% mercerized Egyptian cotton; 205 yd. per 100g skein); color: 2627 French Red; 4 (4, 5, 5, 6) skeins
- US 5 (3.75mm) circular needle, 16" length *(or size needed to match gauge)*
- US 10 (6mm) circular needle, 24" length *(or size needed to match gauge)*

continued ➤

➤ continued

- 0.5"-wide elastic, 20 (21, 22, 23, 23.5)" length
- Stitch markers
- Scrap yarn
- Tapestry needle

GAUGE

20 sts × 28 rows = 4" in St st on smaller needles, unblocked

15 sts × 19 rows = 4" in St st on larger needles, unblocked

SKILLS USED

basic increasing and decreasing

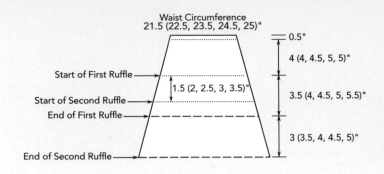

Next round: M1 before each marker.

Rep last 5 rounds 3 (4, 4, 5, 5) more times. 124 (132, 145, 152, 162) sts.

Work even until skirt measures 4 (4, 4.5, 5, 5)" from end of elastic casing.

first ruffle

Switch to larger needles and knit 1 round. Mark this round with a length of scrap yarn or marker.

Next round: Kfb in each st. 248 (264, 290, 304, 324) sts.

Work even for 5.5 (6, 6.5, 7, 7.5)" from start of ruffle.

Next round: K2tog around.124 (132, 145, 152, 162) sts.

Work even for 1.5 (2, 2.5, 3, 3.5)".

Next round: Connect ruffle by picking up the purl bump on the WS of work from the first round of the ruffle (marked with scrap yarn or

marker) and knitting it together with the stitch on the needle. Continue in this manner around until ruffle is joined.

Work even for 1.5 (2, 2.5, 3, 3.5)", marking last round with scrap yarn or st marker.

second ruffle

Next round: Kfb in each st. 248 (264, 290, 304, 324) sts.

Work even for 7.5 (8, 8.5, 9, 9.5)".

Next round: K2tog around. 124 (132, 145, 152, 162) sts.

Work even for 2.5 (3, 3.5, 4, 4.5)".

Next round: Join this ruffle as you did the first.

finishing

Weave in loose ends.

TRIXIE
peasant skirt

TRIXIE
peasant skirt

by carol sulcoski

At age three or so, designer Carol Sulcoski's daughter fell in love with skirts, the twirlier the better. This tiered skirt is designed with her daughter in mind: The soft yarn ensures comfort while the tiers provide extra twirling power. Rows of eyelets are perfect for threading ribbon through, providing a feminine detail to complement the dainty picot hem.

pattern notes

This skirt is knit in the round, from waist to hem. If desired, switch to a circular needle with a longer cable after increasing.

directions

Using smaller circular needle, CO 112 (116, 120, 128, 132) sts. Join for knitting in the round, being careful not to twist sts, and place marker (pm) to indicate beg of round.

Round 1: *K2, p2, rep from * around.

Rep this round until waistband measures 1 (1.25, 1.5, 1.5, 1.5)".

first tier

Knit 1 round.

Next round: Switch to larger needle and knit, increasing 16 (20, 24, 36, 36) sts evenly around. 128 (136, 144, 164, 168) sts.

Continue in St st until skirt measures 2.5 (3.25, 5, 5.5, 7)" from end of ribbing.

Eyelet Round: *K4, yo, k2tog, rep from * around.

Knit 4 rounds.

SIZE
2 (4, 6, 8, 10)

FINISHED MEASUREMENTS
Top hip circumference (measured at top tier): 23.25 (24.75, 26, 30, 30.5)"
Length: 11 (12, 13, 14.5, 16)"

MATERIALS
• Debbie Bliss *Rialto DK* (100% superwash merino wool; 115 yd. per 50g ball); color: 27 Berry; 3 (3, 4, 5, 6) balls

continued >

second tier

Inc Round: *K1, kfb, rep from * around. 192 (204, 216, 246, 252) sts.

Continue in St st for 3".

Eyelet Round: *K4, yo, k2tog, rep from * around.

Knit 4 rounds.

third tier

Inc Round: *K1, kfb, rep from * around. 288 (306, 324, 369, 378) sts.

Continue in St st for 3".

For Size 8 only: Inc 1 st on last round. 288 (306, 324, 370, 378) sts.

create picot edge

Next round: *Yo, k2tog, rep from * to end.

Knit 5 rounds.

BO. Cut yarn, leaving a 6-foot-long tail to sew the hem.

finishing

Turn up picot hem; using long tail and tapestry needle, carefully sew hem to WS of skirt.

Weave in all ends and steam block.

Thread lengths of ribbon through the two eyelet rows and sew ends together, turning in raw edges of ribbon so they do not show.

If you would like to add elastic to the waist, cut the elastic to the child's waist measurement, overlap the two ends by 1" and sew together to form a circle. Pin in place on the WS of the waistband. Using tapestry needle and yarn, trap elastic in place by zigzagging across the elastic, catching purl bumps above and below the elastic. Weave in ends securely.

➤ continued

- US 6 (4mm) circular needle, 16" length *(or size needed to match gauge)*
- US 6 (4mm) circular needle, 24" to 36" length *(optional)*
- US 4 (3.5mm) circular needle, 16" length
- ⅜"-wide grosgrain or satin ribbon, 3 yd.
- Sewing needle and thread to match ribbon
- Stitch marker
- Tapestry needle
- 0.75 (0.75, 1, 1, 1)"-wide elastic, cut to child's waist circumference *(optional)*

GAUGE

22 sts × 28 rows = 4" in St st, on larger needles, unblocked

SKILLS USED

Knitting in the round, basic increasing and decreasing

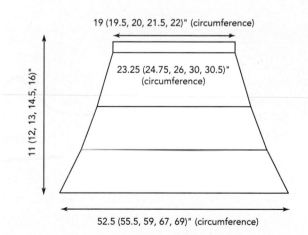

19 (19.5, 20, 21.5, 22)" (circumference)

23.25 (24.75, 26, 30, 30.5)" (circumference)

11 (12, 13, 14.5, 16)"

52.5 (55.5, 59, 67, 69)" (circumference)

SLEEVELESS

MASHENKA
surplice sundress

MASHENKA
surplice sundress

by faina goberstein

T his lovely A–line sundress is knit in the round. The bottom portion is worked in lace using two colors which transitions into wide ribbing in the main color and later, at the empire waist, into stockinette stitch. Crochet edging in the contrast color adorns the top portion of the front. Straps are crocheted in both colors.

pattern notes

This dress is knit in the round from the bottom up to the armholes. At this point, the back is complete. The remainder of the front is worked flat. Crochet edging and the "faux" surplice are added in the contrasting color. The straps are crocheted and sewn to the dress. For all crochet techniques, please refer to the "Special Knitting Techniques" appendix.

The chart in this pattern is available for download at **www.wiley.com/go/moreknittinginthesun**.

double-strand longtail cast-on

Estimate the length of tail needed (you will use about 1 foot of yarn for 20 sts). Use a doubled strand of yarn to make a thick tail this length. Use this tail in the front (around the thumb) and place the working yarn at the back (around the index finger). Work the longtail cast-on as usual (see the "Special Knitting Techniques" appendix). The doubled yarn will produce a thicker edge that serves a decorative purpose and also prevents rolling at the edge.

vine lace pattern

(worked over a multiple of 9 sts in the round)

Round 1: Knit.

Round 2: *Yo, k2, skp, k2tog, k2, yo, k1; rep from * around.

Round 3: Knit.

Round 4: *K2, skp, k2tog, k2, yo, k1, yo; rep from * around.

Rep these 4 rounds for patt.

SIZE
2 (4, 6, 8, 10, 12)

FINISHED MEASUREMENTS
Chest circumference: 24.5 (25.5, 27, 29, 30, 32)"

Length: 19.5 (21, 23, 24, 27, 29)", without straps

MATERIALS
• Debbie Bliss *Baby Cashmerino* (55% wool, 33% microfiber, 12% cashmere; 137 yd. per 50g ball); [MC] color: 100 white, 4 (5, 6, 7, 8, 9) balls; [CC] color: 014 pink, 1 (1, 1, 1, 2, 2) ball(s)

continued ➤

➤ continued

- US 4 (3.5mm) circular needle, 24" length *(or size needed to match gauge)*
- Size E (3.5mm) crochet hook
- Stitch markers
- Tapestry needle
- Sewing needle and thread

GAUGE

25 sts × 34 rows = 4" in St st, blocked

27 sts × 28 rows = 4" in Vine Lace Pattern, blocked

SKILLS USED

Basic increasing and decreasing, lace knitting, intermediate crochet, long-tail cast-on

directions

body

Using circular needle, CC, and double-strand longtail cast-on, CO 198 (207, 216, 234, 243, 261) sts. Place marker (pm) and join to work in the round, being careful not to twist sts.

Knit 1 round.

With MC, begin Vine Lace Pattern starting with Round 2.

Work in Vine Lace Pattern in the following sequence:

>7 rounds with MC
>
>4 rounds with CC
>
>8 rounds with MC
>
>2 rounds with CC
>
>4 rounds with MC

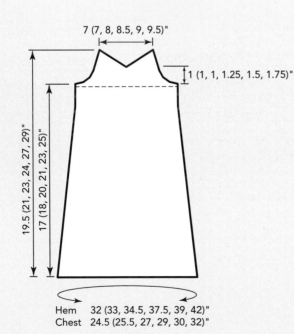

7 (7, 8, 8.5, 9, 9.5)"

1 (1, 1, 1.25, 1.5, 1.75)"

19.5 (21, 23, 24, 27, 29)"

17 (18, 20, 21, 23, 25)"

Hem   32 (33, 34.5, 37.5, 39, 42)"
Chest 24.5 (25.5, 27, 29, 30, 32)"

Vine Lace Pattern Chart

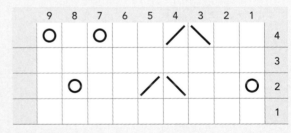

Key to Vine Lace Pattern Chart

☐	**knit** knit stitch
◉	**yo** yarn over
╲	**skp** Slip 1 st knitwise, k1, pass the slipped stitch over the stitch just knit.
╱	**k2tog** Knit 2 sts together as 1 st.

2 rounds with CC

8 rounds with MC

Begin working in rib as follows:

Round 1: *P1, k6, p1, k1; rep from * around.

Rep this round until piece measures 9.5 (10, 10.5, 11, 11.5, 12)" from CO edge.

Dec round: * P1, k2, k2tog, k2, p1, k1; rep from * around. 176 (184, 192, 208, 216, 232) sts.

Next round: * P1, k5, p1, k1; rep from * around.

Rep this round until piece measures 13 (14, 15, 16, 17.5, 19)" from CO edge.

Dec round: * P1, k1, k2tog, k2, p1, k1; rep from * around. 154 (161, 168, 182, 189, 203) sts.

Next round: * P1, k4, p1, k1; rep from * around.

Rep this round until piece measures 14.5 (15.5, 17, 18, 20, 21.5)" from CO edge.

Purl 1 round (First Purl Round).

Knit 3 rounds.

Purl 1 round (Second Purl Round).

Work in St st for 2.75 (3, 3, 3.25, 3.5, 3.75)" more, ending last round 5 (5, 5, 6, 6, 7) sts before marker.

Shape Armholes

NOTE You will place markers where straps will be attached later; leave them in place.

Remove beg of round marker, BO 30 (31, 32, 36, 37, 41) sts, pm (right marker), BO 27 (29, 30, 31, 33, 34) sts, pm (left marker), BO 30 (31, 32, 36, 37, 41) sts, knit rem 67 (70, 74, 79, 82, 87) sts for Front.

Beg working back and forth.

Next row (WS): BO 2 sts, p to end. 65 (68, 72, 77, 80, 85) sts.

Next row: BO 2 sts, k to end. 63 (66, 70, 75, 78, 83) sts.

Rep these 2 rows 0 (0, 0, 1, 1, 1) more time(s). 63 (66, 70, 71, 74, 79) sts.

Purl 1 row.

Dec row (RS): K1, ssk, knit to last 3 sts, k2tog, k1. 61 (64, 68, 69, 72, 77) sts.

Purl 1 row.

Rep Dec row 1 (1, 1, 0, 0, 1) time(s). 59 (62, 66, 69, 72, 75) sts.

Purl 1 row.

Separate for Right and Left Fronts

Next row (RS): K1, ssk, k25 (26, 28, 30, 31, 33), place these sts on holder for left front, BO 3 (4, 4, 3, 4, 3) sts, k25 (26, 28, 30, 31, 33), k2tog, k1. Continue on Right Front only.

right front

Row 1 (WS): P27 (28, 30, 32, 33, 35).

Row 2 (RS): BO 3 sts, knit to last 3 sts, k2tog, k1. 23 (24, 26, 28, 29, 31) sts.

Row 3 and all WS rows: Purl.

Row 4: BO 3 sts, knit to last 3 sts, k2tog, k1. 19 (20, 22, 24, 25, 27) sts.

Row 6: BO 2 sts, knit to last 3 sts, k2tog, k1. 16 (17, 19, 21, 22, 24) sts.

Row 7: Purl.

Rep the last 2 rows 2 (2, 2, 3, 3, 3) more times. 10 (11, 13, 12, 13, 15) sts.

Next row (RS): K1, k2tog, knit to end. 9 (10, 12, 11, 12, 14) sts.

Next row (WS): P1, p2tog, purl to end. 8 (9, 11, 10, 11, 13) sts.

Rep last 2 rows 3 (3, 4, 4, 4, 5) more times. 2 (3, 3, 2, 3, 3) sts.

BO rem sts.

left front

Transfer 27 (28, 30, 32, 33, 35) sts from holder to working needle. With WS facing, join new yarn at V-neck.

Row 1 (WS): P27 (28, 30, 32, 33, 35).

Row 2: K1, ssk, knit to end. 26 (27, 29, 31, 32, 34) sts.

Row 3: BO 3 sts, purl to end. 23 (24, 26, 28, 29, 31) sts.

Rep these 2 rows 1 more time. 19 (20, 22, 24, 25, 27) sts.

Next row: K1, ssk, knit to end. 18 (19, 21, 23, 24, 26) sts.

Next row: BO 2 sts, purl to end. 16 (17, 19, 21, 22, 24) sts.

Rep these 2 rows 2 (2, 2, 3, 3, 3) more times. 10 (11, 13, 12, 13, 15) sts.

Next row (RS): K1, k2tog, knit to end. 9 (10, 12, 11, 12, 14) sts.

Next row (WS): P1, p2tog, purl to end. 8 (9, 11, 10, 11, 13) sts.

Rep last 2 rows 3 (3, 4, 4, 4, 5) more times. 2 (3, 3, 2, 3, 3) sts.

BO rem sts.

finishing

Weave in all ends. Block the finished piece.

empire waist trim

With RS facing, using CC and crochet hook, begin at left "side seam" and Sl st into each purl st of First Purl Round. Fasten off and hide the end.

Continuing with CC and crochet hook, Sl st into each purl st of Second Purl Round. Fasten off and hide the end.

trim around the top

Using sewing needle and contrasting thread, baste a diagonal line down the front that continues the slant of right neckline opening to the Second Purl Round (ending about 2–2.5" left of left seam), place non-removable marker.

Foundation Round: With RS facing, using CC and crochet hook, begin at marker.

Insert the hook front to back through the fabric at basted line, yarn over and pull up a loop. Next insert the hook front to back through the fabric about one stitch length from the first st, yarn over and pull a loop to front and through the first st on the hook (one Sl st complete). Continue making a chain of Sl sts following the basted line; when you reach the neck opening, continue to work Sl sts around the entire top edge of the dress, ending at the bottom of the V-neck.

Next round: Work a second round of Sl st in each st of Foundation Round. Join with Sl st to first st.

Fasten and hide the end.

straps

(make 2)

Foundation Row: With CC and crochet hook, make a chain 8 (10, 11, 12, 13, 14)" long.

Next row: With MC, sc into each ch of Foundation Row.

Next row: With CC, Sl st into each sc.

Fasten and hide the end.

Attach Straps

Sew the completed straps in place as follows, making sure the straps cross in the back:

With RS of strap facing, sew one end to the highest point of right front and the other one at the left marker on the back. Attach the second strap the same way, from the peak of the left front to the right marker on the back.

ANASTASIA
summer dress

ANASTASIA
summer dress

by stacey trock

This adorable dress is fit for a princess on summer vacation . . . beautiful and delicate, but still casual and versatile. Pair the dress with a long sleeve T-shirt underneath, and you can extend its wearing season into autumn and spring. This dress was designed to be as easy to knit as it is to wear: knit in the round so there is minimal finishing, and seed stitch to keep the edges neat without being fussy. A contrasting-color ribbon tied into a bow lends the finishing touch to an effortlessly sweet look.

pattern notes

This dress is constructed from the bottom up and worked in the round so that minimal seaming is required.

The dress is fitted with 1" negative ease. Choose a size approximately 1" smaller than your girl's chest measurement. You can easily adjust the length for taller and shorter girls.

Be sure to swatch in both St st *and* seed st; you may need to use different needle sizes for each.

seed stitch

(worked in the round over an even number of sts)

Round 1: *K1, p1, rep from * around.

Round 2: *P1, k1, rep from * around.

Rep these 2 rounds for seed st.

SIZE
4 (6, 8, 10, 12)

FINISHED MEASUREMENTS
Chest circumference: 22 (24, 25, 27, 29)"
Length: 19.75 (22.25, 26.25, 28.5, 31.25)"

MATERIALS
• Frog Tree *Picoboo* (60% pima cotton, 40% bamboo; 116 yd. per 50g skein); color: 1030 light blue; 4 (6, 7, 8, 9) skeins
• US 5 (3.75mm) circular needle, 16" length for sizes 4–8, 24" length for sizes 10 and 12 (*or size needed to match gauge*)

continued ➤

directions

CO 168 (180, 190, 198, 210) sts. Place contrasting st marker to indicate beg of round. Join to beg working in the round, being careful not to twist sts.

Work in seed st until piece measures 1".

Next round: *Yo, k2tog, rep from * around.

Set-up Round: K18 (20, 22, 24, 26), place marker (pm), k48 (50, 51, 51, 53), pm, k36 (40, 44, 48, 52), pm, k48 (50, 51, 51, 53), pm, k18 (20, 22, 24, 26).

Work 6 (7, 9, 10, 11) rounds even in St st.

Dec Round: *K to m, sm, ssk, knit to 2 sts before next marker, k2tog, sm, rep from *, k to end of round.

➤ continued

- 0.25"-wide ribbon in contrasting color, 2 yd.
- 5 stitch markers, 1 contrasting
- Stitch holder
- Tapestry needle

GAUGE

24 sts × 32 rows = 4" in St st

24 sts × 36 rows = 4" in seed st

Cotton can be stretchy! All measurements are unblocked, made without stretching the fabric. To measure, let knitted piece lay naturally.

SKILLS USED

Basic increasing and decreasing, simple stitch patterns

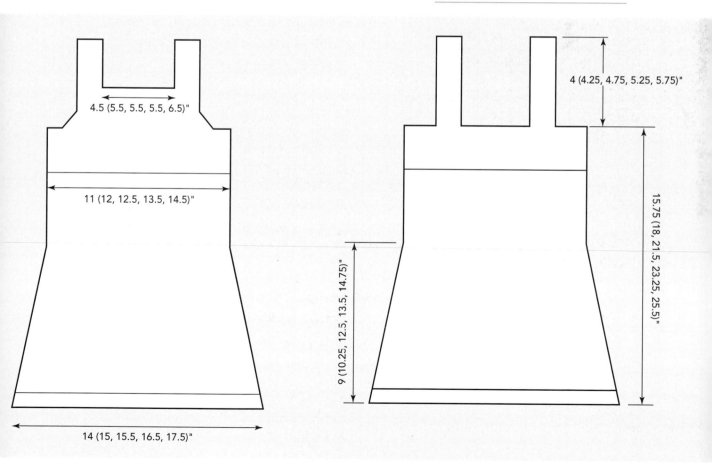

4.5 (5.5, 5.5, 5.5, 6.5)"

11 (12, 12.5, 13.5, 14.5)"

14 (15, 15.5, 16.5, 17.5)"

9 (10.25, 12.5, 13.5, 14.75)"

4 (4.25, 4.75, 5.25, 5.75)"

15.75 (18, 21.5, 23.25, 25.5)"

Rep these 7 (8, 10, 11, 12) rounds 8 more times. 132 (144, 154, 162, 174) sts. Piece will measure approximately 9 (10.25, 12.5, 13.5, 14.75)".

Continue to work in St st for 5 (5.5, 6, 6.5, 7)" more. If your little one is taller or shorter than average, this is the ideal point to either lengthen or shorten the dress. Refer to the schematic for measurements.

Next round: *Yo, k2tog, rep from * around.

Work in seed st for 1.5 (2, 2.75, 3, 3.5)".

Next round: Work 60 (72, 72, 81, 88) sts in seed st. BO purlwise 71 (71, 81, 80, 85) sts. You should now be at the beg of round marker with one loop on your RH needle.

You will now begin working back and forth, maintaining the seed st patt.

Set-up Row: Remove marker, BO 9 (15, 11, 17, 19) sts, ssk, work in patt to last 3 sts, k2tog, work 1. 50 (56, 60, 63, 68) sts rem.

Next row (WS): Work patt.

Dec Row (RS): Work 1 in patt, ssk, work in patt to 3 sts before end of row, k2tog, work 1.

Next row (WS): Work patt.

Rep these 2 rows 2 (2, 3, 3, 3) more times. 44 (50, 52, 55, 60) sts.

Continue to work in seed st until piece measures 2.25 (2.5, 2.75, 3, 3.25)" from BO, ending with a WS row.

straps

To work straps, continue in seed st patt.

Set-up Row (RS): Work 10 (10, 12, 12, 12) sts, and place these sts on a holder. BO purlwise 24 (30, 28, 31, 36) sts, work rem 10 (10, 12, 12, 12) sts. You will have 2 sets of 10 (10, 12, 12, 12) sts.

Work first strap in seed st for 6 (6.25, 7, 7.75, 8.25)", ending on a WS. BO purlwise.

Return held sts to needles. Join new yarn, and work this strap the same way as the first strap.

finishing

With tapestry needle and spare piece of yarn, attach BO edge of the first strap to BO edge at back of dress. Attach the second strap in the same manner.

Using a tapestry needle, thread ribbon through eyelets at the waistline of the dress. Tie a pretty bow! To finish the ends of the ribbon nicely, trim at a diagonal. If your ribbon is polyester, you can singe the tips of the ribbon with a lighted match to keep the ribbon from unraveling.

WENDY
pleated empire top
by tian connaughton

This is a simple empire-waisted top worked from the bottom up. It blends comfort and practicality with touches of girly femininity. This cute top is perfect with shorts or worn over a top and leggings on cooler days.

pattern notes

For the larger sizes, you may wish to start the project on a longer circular needle. For all crochet techniques, please refer to the "Special Knitting Techniques" appendix.

leaf panel

(worked in the round over 19 sts)

Round 1: K7, k2tog, yo, k1, yo, skp, k7.

Round 2 and all even rounds: Knit.

Round 3: K6, k2tog, yo, k3, yo, skp, k6.

Round 5: K5, k2tog, yo, k5, yo, skp, k5.

Round 7: K4, k2tog, yo, k7, yo, skp, k4.

Round 9: K3, k2tog, yo, k9, yo, skp, k3.

Round 11: K2, k2tog, yo, k11, yo, skp, k2.

Round 13: K1, k2tog, yo, k13, yo, skp, k1.

Round 15: Knit.

Round 16: K10, *insert crochet hook into yo from front to back (begin with first yo of Round 13), bring yarn around hook, draw loop through to RS and place it on RH needle, taking care not to pull loop too tight; rep from * into *each* of the rem yarn overs of leaf from right to left (14 loops on needle); knit last 9 sts.

Round 17: K9, knit tog the 14 loops with next st, k9.

Round 18: Knit.

SIZE
2 (4, 6, 8, 10, 12)

FINISHED MEASUREMENTS
Chest circumference: 20 (22, 24, 25.5, 27, 29)"
Length: 15.5 (17, 19, 20.5, 22.5, 23)"

MATERIALS
• Cascade *Ultra Pima* (100% pima cotton; 220yd. per 100g skein); color: 3740 Sprout; 2 (2, 3, 3, 4, 4) skeins

continued ➤

directions

You will begin working the skirt from the bottom up in the round. You may wish to work on a shorter needle once you reach the bodice.

skirt

With circular needle, CO 162 (170, 186, 202, 214, 226) sts. Place marker (pm), and join for working in the round, being careful not to twist sts.

Rounds 1–3: Knit.

Round 4: Purl.

Rep these 4 rounds twice more.

Work even in St st until piece measures 2.5".

Next round: K31 (33, 37, 41, 44, 47), pm, work Leaf Panel patt over 19 sts beg with Round 1, pm, k31, (33, 37, 41, 44, 47), pm, k to end of round.

*Keeping center panel in patt and rem sts in St st, work through Round 18 of Leaf Panel.

Work 6 rounds even in St st.

➤ continued

- US 5 (3.75mm) circular needle, 24" length *(or size needed to match gauge)*
- Size D (3.25mm) crochet hook
- Cable needle
- Tapestry needle
- Scrap yarn or stitch holder

GAUGE
24 sts × 32 rows = 4" in St st

SKILLS USED
Basic increasing and decreasing, simple crochet edging, lace knitting

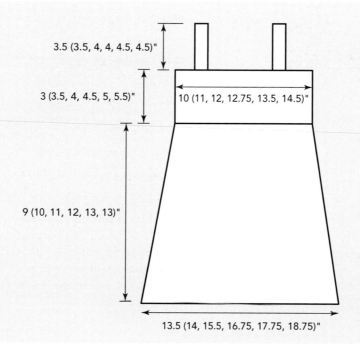

3.5 (3.5, 4, 4, 4.5, 4.5)"

3 (3.5, 4, 4.5, 5, 5.5)"

10 (11, 12, 12.75, 13.5, 14.5)"

9 (10, 11, 12, 13, 13)"

13.5 (14, 15.5, 16.75, 17.75, 18.75)"

Rep the previous 24 rounds 1 (1, 2, 2, 2, 2) time(s) more.

Continue in St st until piece measures 9 (10, 11, 12, 13, 13)".

pleats

On the next round you will make 6 pleats across the front to transition from skirt to bodice; you will also make decreases across the back.

Front: K4 (6, 8, 4, 5, 8); **sl next 3 (3, 3, 4, 4, 4) sts to cable needle (CN) and hold to *front*, k sts from CN tog with next 3 (3, 3, 4, 4, 4) sts from working needle; sl next 3 (3, 3, 4, 4, 4) sts to CN and hold to *back*, k next 3 (3, 3, 4, 4, 4) sts from working needle tog with sts from CN**; k6, sl next 9 (9, 10, 12, 13, 13) sts to CN and hold to *front*, k sts from CN tog with next 9 (9, 10, 12, 13, 13) sts on working needle; k1; sl next 9 (9, 10, 12, 13, 13) sts to CN and hold to *back*, k next 9 (9, 10, 12, 13, 13) sts on working needle tog with sts from CN; k6; rep from ** to ** once; k4 (6, 8, 4, 5, 8); 57 (61, 67, 69, 73, 79) sts for front.

Back: K6 (3, 1, 2, 2, 5), *k2tog, k2 (4, 4, 4, 4, 4), rep from * 17 (13, 15, 16, 17, 17) times, k2tog, k5 (3, 1, 2, 2, 5); 63 (71, 77, 84, 89, 95) sts for back. 120 (132, 144, 153, 162, 174) sts.

bodice

Round 1: Purl.

Rounds 2–4: Knit.

Round 5: Purl.

Rep Rounds 2–5 until bodice measures 3 (3.5, 4, 4.5, 5, 5.5)".

BO knitwise.

straps

(make 2)

CO 12 sts.

Beg with a knit row, work in St st for 7 (7, 8, 8, 9, 9)".

BO and break yarn.

finishing
crochet scallop edge

With WS facing, attach yarn with a Sl st, work 1 row of sc along one long side of strap.

Turn, ch1, *skip first sc, work 4 hdc in next st, skip next st, sc in next st, skip next st; rep from * to end.

Fasten off.

Work second side of strap the same. Rep for second strap.

Hem: With RS facing, attach yarn with Sl st. *Skip first st, work 4 hdc in next st, skip next st, sc in next st; rep from * to last st. Fasten off.

With piece lying flat, attach straps and weave in all ends. Block, folding large pleats over leaf panel.

HERMIONE

sun top

by janine le cras

This pretty little sun top is knit in a beautiful super-wash merino finished with cute ribbon bows—perfect for a special occasion without being too formal. Paired with the Ginny shrug, it's a sure winner in all seasons.

pattern notes

Knit in the round from the bottom up, the shaping of the top is achieved by changing to a smaller needle rather than reducing the number of stitches. Check your gauge on the largest and smallest needles before knitting.

To work garter st in the round, alternate knit and purl rounds.

The chart in this pattern is available for download at **www.wiley.com/go/moreknittinginthesun**.

directions

skirt

Using largest circular needle, CO 128 (144,160, 176, 184, 192) sts. Join in the round being careful not to twist sts.

Work 5 rounds in garter st.

Beg Hermione Lace patt with Round 1 of the chart or following the written instructions below. You will work 16 (18, 20, 22, 23, 24) reps of the lace patt around the garment.

SIZE
2 (4, 6, 8, 10, 12)

FINISHED MEASUREMENTS
Chest circumference: 20 (22, 24.5, 27, 28, 29.5)"

Length to underarm: 9.25 (9.75, 11.5, 13, 14, 15.5)"

MATERIALS
• Madelinetosh *Tosh Sock* (100% superwash merino wool; 395 yd. per 110g skein); color: Tomato; 1 (1, 1, 2, 2, 2) skein(s)

continued ➤

Hermione Lace Chart

8	7	6	5	4	3	2	1	
								16
sk2p	O						O	15
								14
		O	/		\	O		13
								12
	O	/			\		O	11
								10
O						\		9
								8
		O	sk2p	O				7
								6
	\	O			O	/		5
								4
		\	O		O	/		3
								2
			\	O				1

Key to Hermione Lace Chart

☐ **knit**
knit stitch

O **yo**
yarn over

\ **ssk**
Slip 1 stitch as if to knit.
Slip another stitch as if to knit. Insert LH needle into front of these 2 stitches and knit them together.

/ **k2tog**
Knit 2 stitches together as 1 stitch.

λ **sk2p**
Slip 1, k2tog, pass slip stitch over k2tog.

➤ **continued**

- US 3 (3.25mm) needles (or size needed to match gauge)
- US 7 (4.5mm) circular needle, 24" length (or size needed to match gauge)
- US 6 (4mm) circular needle, 24" length
- 1"-wide ribbon, 1 yd.
- Scrap yarn or stitch holder
- Tapestry needle

GAUGE

26 sts × 36 rows = 4" in St st on smallest needles, blocked

20 sts × 32 rows = 4" over lace pattern on largest needles, blocked

SKILLS USED

Basic increasing and decreasing, easy lace knitting, knitting in the round

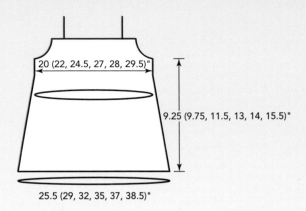

20 (22, 24.5, 27, 28, 29.5)"

9.25 (9.75, 11.5, 13, 14, 15.5)"

25.5 (29, 32, 35, 37, 38.5)"

Hermione Lace Pattern

Round 1: *K3, yo, ssk, k3, rep from *.

Round 2 and all even rounds: Knit.

Round 3: *K1, k2tog, yo, k1, yo, ssk, k2, rep from *.

Round 5: *K2tog, yo, k3, yo, ssk, k1, rep from *.

Round 7: *K2, yo, sk2p, yo, k3, rep from *.

Round 9: *Ssk, k6, yo, rep from *.

Round 11: *Yo, ssk, k3, k2tog, yo, k1, rep from *.

Round 13: *K1, yo, ssk, k1, k2tog, yo, k2, rep from *.

Round 15: *Yo, k5, yo, sk2p, rep from *.

Round 16: Knit.

Rep Rounds 1–16 for patt.

Continue in Hermione Lace patt as set, and when the work measures 4 (4, 4.5, 4.5, 4.5, 5)" from CO edge, change to needles one size smaller. Continue in lace patt until work measures 8 (8, 9, 9, 9, 10)" from the CO edge.

Change to smallest needles and work 3 rounds in garter st.

Switch to St st and work even for 1.25 (1.75, 2.5, 4, 5, 5.5)". The top now measures 9.25 (9.75, 11.5, 13, 14, 15.5)".

front

You will now shape the armholes in the front and complete the bodice.

K64 (72, 80, 88, 92, 96) sts and place them on scrap yarn or a holder. Continue working back and forth in St st on the sts rem on the needle.

BO 3 (3, 4, 4, 5, 5) sts at beg of next 2 rows.

BO 2 (3, 3, 4, 4, 4) sts at beg of next 2 rows.

BO 1 st at beg of next 2 rows.

Continue working in St st for 1 (1, 1.5, 2, 2, 2.5)" more.

Work 5 rows in garter st.

BO rem 52 (58, 64, 70, 72, 76) sts.

Transfer held sts back to working needle and work as for front.

finishing

Block to the dimensions given in the schematic. Weave in all ends. Cut the ribbon into 4 equal lengths and sew one piece to each side of the top as shown on the schematic. Tie each pair into a bow.

RAMONA
racerback tank

by katherine vaughan

This simple camisole avoids ruffles and lace, and the racerback styling stays on a girl's shoulders even when she's swinging from the trees. The purled diamonds echo the lace pattern from the Beezus cardigan, making them a perfect twinset.

pattern notes

This pattern uses a single crochet edging around the armholes and hem. If you are more comfortable with attached I-cord than crochet, it can be used as a slightly bulkier substitute. For I-cord and I-cord bind-off, as well as crochet techniques, please refer to the "Special Knitting Techniques" appendix.

The chart in this pattern is available for download at **www.wiley.com/go/moreknittinginthesun**.

ramona stitch

(worked over a multiple of 6 sts + 3)

Row 1 and all WS rows: Purl.

Row 2: K1, *p1, k5, rep from * to last 2 sts, p1, k1.

Row 4: *P1, K1, p1, k3, rep from * to last 3 sts, p1, k1, p1.

Row 6: K1, *p1, k5, rep from * to last 2 sts, p1, k1.

Row 8: K4, *p1, k5, rep from * to last 5 sts, p1, k4.

Row 10: *K3, p1, k1, p1, rep from * to last 3 sts, k3.

Row 12: K4, *p1, k5, rep from * to last 5 sts, p1, k4.

Rep these 12 rows for patt.

SIZE
2 (4, 6, 8, 10, 12)

FINISHED MEASUREMENTS
Chest circumference: 19 (21, 23, 24.5, 26, 28)"

Length to underarm: 8.5 (9, 9.5, 11, 12, 12.5)"

MATERIALS
- Classic Elite *Allegoro* (70% organic cotton, 30% linen; 152 yd. per 50g skein); color: 5634 Best Berry; 1 (2, 2, 3, 3, 3) skein(s)
- US 3 (3.25mm) straight needles *(or size needed to match gauge)*
- US 3 (3.25mm) double-pointed needles

continued ➤

Ramona Stitch Chart

			●					12
11								
		●		●				10
9								
			●					8
7								
	●				●			6
5								
●		●		●		●		4
3								
●				●				2
1								

Key to Ramona Stitch Chart

▢ **knit**
RS: knit stitch
WS: purl stitch

▣ **purl**
RS: purl stitch
WS: knit stitch

➤ continued

- Size D (3.25mm) crochet hook
- Stitch holder
- Tapestry needle

GAUGE

25 sts × 39 rows = 4" in St st, blocked

25 sts × 39 rows = 4" in Ramona Stitch, blocked

SKILLS USED

Knit and purl stitch, basic shaping, I-cord and I-cord bind-off, single crochet edging, seaming

directions
back

CO 61 (67, 73, 75, 83, 89) sts.

Next row (WS): P2 (2, 2, 3, 1, 1), work Ramona Stitch beg with Row 1 (a WS row), end p2 (2, 2, 3, 1, 1).

Next row (RS): K2, (2, 2, 3, 1, 1), work Ramona Stitch to last 2 (2, 2, 3, 1, 1) st(s), k to end.

Continue in Ramona Stitch as set until Back measures 8.5 (9, 9.5, 11, 12, 12.5)" from CO edge, ending with a WS row.

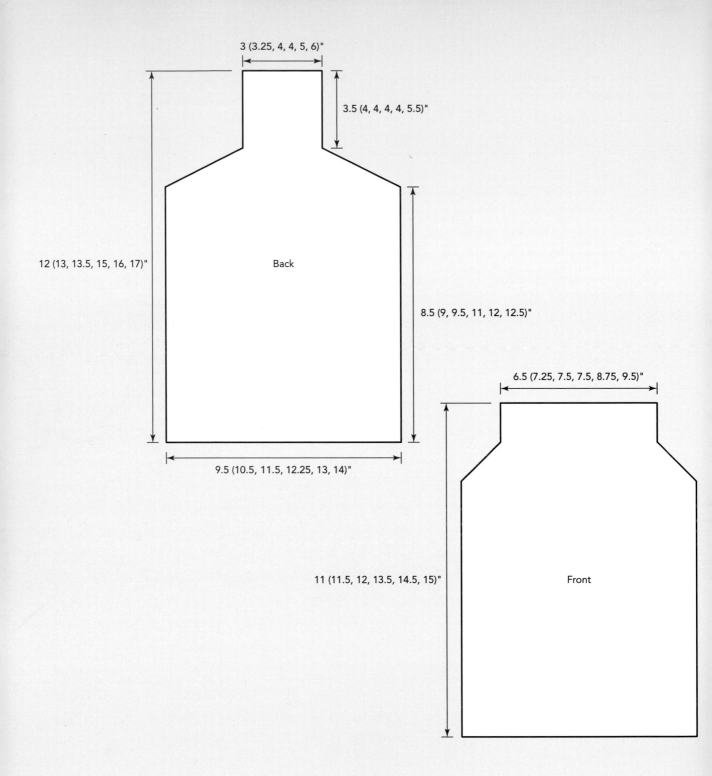

3 (3.25, 4, 4, 5, 6)"

3.5 (4, 4, 4, 4, 5.5)"

12 (13, 13.5, 15, 16, 17)"

Back

8.5 (9, 9.5, 11, 12, 12.5)"

9.5 (10.5, 11.5, 12.25, 13, 14)"

6.5 (7.25, 7.5, 7.5, 8.75, 9.5)"

11 (11.5, 12, 13.5, 14.5, 15)"

Front

Shape Armholes

Continue in Ramona Stitch throughout, keeping patt aligned.

Rows 1 and 2: BO 6, work to end. 49 (55, 61, 63, 71, 77) sts.

Rows 3 and 4: BO 4 (5, 5, 5, 6, 6), work to end. 41 (45, 51, 53, 59, 65) sts.

Rows 5 and 6: BO 4, (5, 5, 6, 6, 6), work to end. 33 (35, 41, 41, 47, 53) sts.

Rows 7 and 8: BO 3, work to end. 27 (29, 35, 35, 41, 47) sts.

Rows 9 and 10: BO 2, work to end. 23 (25, 31, 31, 37, 43) sts.

Rows 11 and 12: BO 2, work to end. 19 (21, 27, 27, 33, 39) sts.

Rows 13 and 14: BO 1, work to end. 17 (19, 25, 25, 31, 37) sts.

Work even in Ramona Stitch until Back measures 12 (13, 13.5, 15, 16, 17)" from CO edge, ending with a WS row.

Place rem sts on holder and set aside.

front

CO 61 (67, 73, 75, 83, 89) sts. Work Front same as Back to beg of armhole shaping.

Shape Armholes

Continue in Ramona Stitch, keeping patt aligned.

Rows 1 and 2: BO 4 (5, 5, 6, 6, 6), work to end. 53 (57, 63, 63, 71, 77) sts.

Rows 3 and 4: BO 3 (3, 4, 4, 4, 5), work to end. 47 (51, 55, 55, 63, 67) sts.

Rows 5 and 6: BO 2 (2, 3, 3, 3, 3), work to end. 43 (47, 49, 49, 57, 61) sts.

Rows 7 and 8: BO 1, work to end. 41 (45, 47, 47, 55, 59) sts.

Work even in patt until Front measures 11 (11.5, 12, 13.5, 14.5, 15)" from CO edge, ending with a WS row.

straps

CO 3 sts, then, using dpns, work I-cord bind-off across Front sts. When 3 sts rem on the needle, switch to I-cord.

Work I-cord for 3 (3.5, 4.5, 5, 6, 7)" for right strap.

Transfer Back sts from holder to dpn.

Continue from I-cord strap to I-cord bind-off across back sts. When 3 sts rem, switch to I-cord for the left strap.

Work I-cord for 3 (3.5, 4.5, 5, 6, 7)".

BO rem sts.

Sew BO edge to left front to complete left strap.

finishing

Sew side seams.

Using crochet hook, work single crochet edging around armholes and hem.

Weave in ends and trim.

Block.

PIPPI
lacy collared top

PIPPI
lacy collared top

by mary c. gildersleeve

This sun-baked, terra cotta–colored top will keep your girl cool in the hottest weather. Knit in a washable cotton blend, this top is fun to knit with its budding flowers and sunbeam lace collar. It's the perfect knit for your own active Pippi!

pattern notes

This top is knit in the round from hem to underarm. The back is finished in stockinette stitch with self-finishing seed stitch borders. A gentle V-neck completes the front. The lace collar is knit from stitches picked up around the neck.

When knitting back and forth, always slip the first stitch as if to purl to ensure an even pick-up edge. This selvedge stitch is included in the stitch counts given in the directions.

For three-needle bind-off, picking up stitches, and cast-on methods, please refer to the "Special Knitting Techniques" appendix.

All the charts in this pattern are available for download at **www.wiley.com/go/moreknittinginthesun**.

budding flower lace pattern

Refer to the legend for instructions on working the "Left Twist."

Round 1: *K1, yo, skp, k7, k2tog, yo, rep from * to end.

Rounds 2, 4, 6, 8, 10, 12, 14, 16, & 18: Knit.

Round 3: *K2, yo, skp, k5, k2tog, yo, k1, rep from * to end.

Round 5: *K3, yo, skp, k3, k2tog, yo, k2, rep from * to end.

Round 7: *K4, yo, skp, k1, k2tog, yo, k3, rep from * to end.

Round 9: *K1, yo, skp, k2, yo, s2kp, yo, k2, k2tog, yo, rep from * to end.

SIZE

2 (4, 6, 8, 10, 12)

FINISHED MEASUREMENTS

Hem circumference: 30 (33, 36, 39, 42, 45)"

Chest circumference: 17.5 (19.25, 21, 22.75, 24.5, 26.5)", unstretched

Length: 11 (13, 15, 17, 19, 20)"

MATERIALS

• Lion Brand *Cotton-Ease* (50% cotton, 50% acrylic; 207 yd. per 100g skein); color: 134 Terracotta; 2 (2, 2, 3, 3, 4) skeins

• US 8 (5mm) circular needle, 24" length (*or size needed to match gauge*)

continued ➤

- US 4 (3.5mm) circular needle, 24" length
- *Smallest sizes might need 16" length needles*
- US 4 (3.5mm) double-pointed needles, 7" length
- Tapestry needle
- Stitch holders, 3 or more, or scrap yarn

GAUGE

18 sts × 22 rows = 4" in St st on larger needles, unblocked

12 sts × 48 rows = 3" × 8" in Budding Flower Lace pattern on larger needles, blocked

SKILLS USED

Lace knitting, knitting in the round, chart reading, picking up stitches, three-needle bind-off

Round 11: Rep Round 3.

Round 13: Rep Round 5.

Round 15: Rep Round 7.

Round 17: *K5, yo, s2kp, yo, k4, rep from * to end.

Round 19: *K3, k2tog, yo, Left Twist, k1, yo, skp, k2, rep from * to end.

Round 20: *K6, Left Twist, k4, rep from * to end.

Rounds 21–34: Rep Rounds 19 and 20.

Round 35: *K2, k2tog, yo, k5, yo, skp, k1, rep from * to end.

Round 36 and foll even rows: Knit.

Round 37: *K1, k2tog, yo, k7, yo, skp, rep from * to end.

Round 39: *K1, yo, skp, k3, yo, skp, k2, k2tog, yo, rep from * to end.

Round 41: *K2, yo, skp, k2tog, yo, k1, yo, skp, k2tog, yo, k1, rep from * to end.

Round 43: Rep Round 5.

Round 45: Rep Round 7.

Round 47: Rep Round 17.

directions

With larger circular needle, CO 120 (132, 144, 156, 168, 180). Join, being careful not to twist sts, and place marker (pm). Marker indicates center back.

Purl 1 round.

Begin Budding Flower Lace Chart with Round 1. You will work the 12 sts of the chart 10 (11, 12, 13, 14, 15) times around.

Work only the rounds specified below for your size.

For Size 2: Work Rounds 1–8, 17–22, then 35–48.

For Size 4: Work Rounds 1–22, then 35–48.

For all other sizes: Work Rounds 1–48. For additional length below the empire waist, work additional rep of rounds 19–20.

Piece measures approximately 5 (6.25, 8, 8, 8, 8)".

Budding Flower Lace Chart

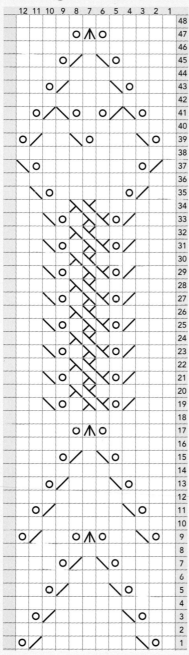

Sunbeam Edging Chart

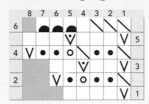

Key to charts

V	**slip**	slip stitch as if to purl.
☐	**knit**	RS: knit stitch WS: purl stitch
▨	**No Stitch**	
╲	**skp**	Slip 1, knit 1, pass slipped stitch over.
●	**purl**	RS: purl stitch WS: knit stitch
○	**yo**	yarn over
Ⅴ	**(k1, p1, k1) in 1 st**	Knit, purl, and knit again all in the same st to make 3 sts from 1.
◗	**Bind Off**	
╱	**k2tog**	Knit 2 stitches together as 1 stitch.
⋀	**s2kp**	Slip 2 sts as if to k2tog, k1, pass the 2 slipped sts over the st just knit.
⋋⋌	**left twist**	Sl1 to CN, hold in front. K1, k1 from CN.

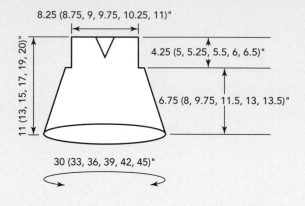

8.25 (8.75, 9, 9.75, 10.25, 11)"

4.25 (5, 5.25, 5.5, 6, 6.5)"

11 (13, 15, 17, 19, 20)"

6.75 (8, 9.75, 11.5, 13, 13.5)"

30 (33, 36, 39, 42, 45)"

Change to smaller circular needle and begin ribbing as follows: k2, *p3, k3, rep from *, ending p3, k1. Work ribbing for 1 (1, 1, 2, 2.5, 3)".

Dec Round: *K2, p2tog, p1, k3, p3tog, k1, rep from * around. 90 (99, 108, 117, 126, 135) sts rem.

Next round: Continue in rib as follows: *K2, p2, k3, p1, k1, rep from * to end.

Rep this round for .75 (.75, .75, 1.5, 2.5, 2.5)".

divide front and back

Change to larger needles and k18 (21, 23, 25, 27, 30), BO 8 for underarm, k37 (41, 46, 50, 55, 59) and move these sts to holder or scrap yarn for front, BO 8 for underarm, k19 (21, 23, 26, 28, 30). Break yarn and slip these 19 (21, 23, 26, 28, 30) sts back to LH needle; 37 (42, 46, 51, 55, 60) sts on needle for Back.

back

Rejoin yarn with RS facing, work 5 sts in seed st, pm, k27 (32, 36, 41, 45, 50), pm, work 5 sts in seed st.

Next row (WS): Maintain 5 sts on each edge in seed st and work St st between markers.

Next 3 RS rows: Seed st 5, ssk, k to 2 sts before marker, k2tog, seed st 5. 31 (36, 40, 45, 49, 54) sts.

Keeping first and last 5 sts in seed st, work even in St st on sts between markers until Back measures 3.75 (4.5, 4.75, 5, 5.5, 6)" from armhole BO, ending with a WS row.

Right Shoulder

Maintaining patt, work 8 (9, 11, 13, 15, 16) sts; turn and work back. Continue on these 8 (9, 11, 13, 15, 16) sts only as est for 4 more rows. Armhole will measure approximately 4.25 (5, 5.25, 5.5, 6, 6.5)". Break yarn and slip these sts to stitch holder or scrap yarn for shoulder.

Back Neck

Slip center 15 (18, 18, 19, 19, 22) sts to second holder or scrap yarn for neck.

Left Shoulder

Reattach yarn at neck edge and continue in patt over rem 8 (9, 11, 13, 15, 16) sts for 6 rows. Break yarn and slip these sts to holder or scrap yarn.

front

Work as for Back until piece measures 1.5", ending with a WS row, then divide for neck opening.

Left Front

Next row (RS): Maintaining patt, work across 14 (16, 19, 21, 23, 25) sts; turn.

Next row (WS): Sl 1, p to last 5 sts, seed st 5.

Next row (RS): Seed st 5, k to last 3 sts, k2tog, k1.

Rep the last 2 rows until 8 (9, 11, 13, 15, 16) sts rem.

Work even until the left front measures the same as the back to the shoulder. Use the three-needle bind-off to attach the front and back left shoulders.

Center Neck
Place 3 (2, 2, 3, 3, 2) sts on holder for neck.

Right Front
With RS facing, attach yarn at neck edge and k across to last 5 sts, seed st to end.

Next row: Seed st 5, p to end.

Next row: Sl 1, skp, k to last 5 sts, seed st to end.

Rep the last 2 rows until 8 (9, 11, 13, 15, 16) sts rem.

Work even until the right front measures the same as the back to the shoulder. Use the three-needle bind-off to attach the front and back right shoulders.

collar

With smaller needles and RS facing, starting at center front: Slip first 2 (1, 1, 2, 2, 1) sts from neck st holder to RH needle, join yarn and k1 from neck st holder, pick up and knit 16 (18, 18, 20, 22, 22) sts along right neck, 15 (18, 18, 19, 19, 22) sts held for back neck, pick up and knit 16 (18, 18, 20, 21, 22) sts along left neck edge, k2 (1, 1, 2, 2, 1) sts from holder. 50 (56, 56, 62, 65, 68) sts. If you have made any changes to the neck-line shaping, you will need a multiple of 3, plus 2 sts. DO NOT JOIN. The collar is worked back and forth in garter st.

Next row (WS): *Kfb, rep from * to last st, k1. 109 (115, 115, 127, 133, 139) sts.

Work in garter st for 12 rows (6 ridges), ending with a WS row.

Switch to dpns and work Sunbeam Edging to complete collar as follows:

Set-up Row: CO 5 sts using backward loop or knitted cast-on, k4, skp last st with first live st from collar.

Begin Sunbeam Edging by following the chart or the written instructions below. On RS rows, the final skp will join 1 edging st with 1 st from collar.

Row 1: Sl 1, k4.

Row 2: Sl1, k1, yo, k2, skp last st with collar st.

Row 3: Sl1, k2, [k1, p1, k1 in next st], k2.

Row 4: Sl1, k2, yo, skp, k2, skp last st with collar st.

Row 5: Sl1, k3, [k1, p1, k1, in next st], k3.

Row 6: BO 3, k1, skp, skp, skp last st with collar st.

Rep Rows 1–6 until all collar sts are consumed.

BO rem 5 sts.

finishing

Weave in ends.

CHARLIE
updated argyle vest

CHARLIE
updated argyle vest
by kristi porter

This vest is a classic handknit updated for modern appeal! A soft—and washable—hand-dyed yarn and a bold intarsia pattern that resembles argyle make this vest a fresh choice while adding a bit of warmth and style to your child's wardrobe.

pattern notes

Intarsia: Work each color section with a separate length (or bobbin) of yarn. Be sure to twist the two strands of yarn around each other when switching between colors to avoid gaps.

For three-needle bind-off, picking up stitches, and the s2kp decrease, please refer to the "Special Knitting Techniques" appendix.

All the charts in this pattern are available for download at **www.wiley.com/go/moreknittinginthesun**.

directions
back

Using smaller needles and MC, CO 65 (69, 75, 79, 85) sts.

Work in k1, p1 rib for 1 (1, 1, 1.5, 1.5)" ending with a RS row.

Switch to larger needles and St st and work even until back measures 7 (8, 9, 10.5, 11.5)" from CO edge, ending with a WS row.

Shape Armholes

BO 6 (6, 7, 8, 8) sts at beg of next 2 rows. 53 (57, 61, 63, 69) sts.

Dec Row (RS): K1, ssk, k to last 3 sts, k2tog, k1.

SIZE
2 (4, 6, 8, 10)

FINISHED MEASUREMENTS
Chest circumference: 26 (28, 30, 32, 34)"
Length: 12 (13.5, 15, 17, 18.5)"

MATERIALS
- Alchemy Yarns *Temple* (100% superfine merino wool; 128 yd. per 50g skein); [MC] Lulu Brown, 2 (3, 3, 4, 4) skeins; [CC1] Joshua Tree, 1 skein; [CC2] Dragon, 1 skein; [CC3] Citrine, 1 skein
- US 5 (3.75mm) straight needles (*or size needed to match gauge*)
- US 3 (3.25mm) straight needles

continued ➤

> continued

- US 3 (3.25mm) circular needle, 16" length, or double-pointed needles
- Bobbins, optional
- Stitch holder or scrap yarn
- Tapestry needle
- Safety pin

GAUGE

20 sts × 28 rows = 4" in St st on larger needles, blocked

SKILLS USED

Intarsia, basic decreasing, picking up stitches, three-needle bind-off

Rep Dec Row every RS row 4 (5, 6, 6, 7) times more. 43 (45, 47, 49, 53) sts.

Work even until back measures 5 (5.5, 6, 6.5, 7)" from beg of armhole shaping. Put all sts on holder or scrap yarn.

front

Using smaller needles and MC, CO 65 (69, 75, 79, 85) sts.

Work in k1, p1 rib for 1 (1, 1, 1.5, 1.5)" ending with a RS row.

Set-up Row (WS): P22 (24, 24, 36, 29), place marker (pm), p21 (21, 27, 27, 27), pm, p to end.

Working in St st, work in MC outside the markers and begin following the Argyle Chart between markers.

Use Argyle Chart A for sizes 2 and 4; use Argyle Chart B for sizes 6, 8, and 10.

Work even until back measures 7 (8, 9, 10.5, 11.5)" from CO edge, ending with a WS row.

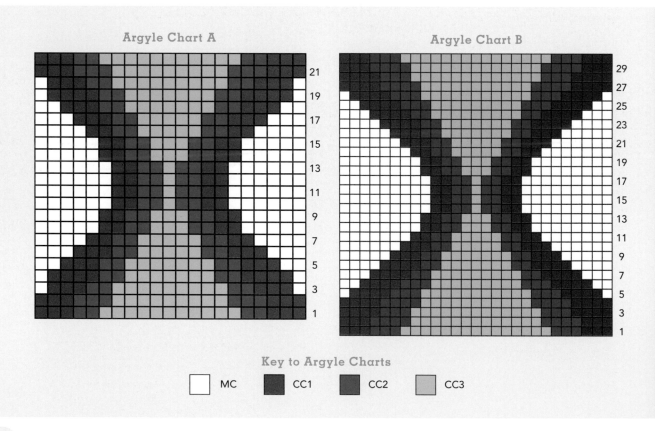

Argyle Chart A — **Argyle Chart B**

Key to Argyle Charts

☐ MC ■ CC1 ■ CC2 ■ CC3

Shape Armholes and Neckline

NOTE You will begin shaping the armholes, and then shape the neck. You will work both shapings simultaneously, so read through this whole section before continuing.

BO 6 (6, 7, 8, 8) sts at beg of next 2 rows.

Dec Row (RS): K1, ssk, k to last 3 sts, k2tog, k1.

Rep Dec Row every RS row 4 (5, 6, 6, 7) times more.

At the same time, when front measures 0.5 (1, 1, 1, 1)" from beg of armhole shaping, beg shaping the neck.

Next RS row: Work armhole dec, k in patt to center st, place center st on safety pin, attach a second piece of CC3 yarn if needed, k to end of row, working armhole dec as set.

Next row: Purl in patt, working each side of neck separately.

Next row (RS): Work armhole dec if necessary, work in patt to 3 sts before center st, ssk, k1; on left side of neck, k1, k2tog, k to end of row, working armhole dec if necessary.

Rep these 2 rows 10 (11, 12, 13, 14) times more. 10 (10, 10, 10, 11) sts rem for each shoulder.

Work even until each side measures 5 (5.5, 6, 6.5, 7)" from beg of armhole shaping.

finishing

Hold front and back with RS tog. Use the three-needle bind-off to attach the 10 (10, 10, 10, 11) shoulder sts, k across 23 (25, 27, 29, 31) sts on holder for back neck, use three-needle bind-off to attach the rem 10 (10, 10, 10, 11) shoulder sts. Place back neck sts on holder.

Weave in ends. Block piece to measurements given in schematic.

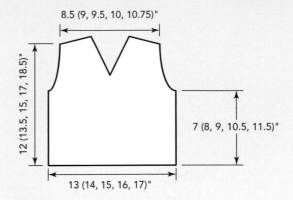

Using smaller needles and MC, begin at left front underarm and pick up and knit 66 (70, 76, 82, 90) sts around armhole opening. Work back and forth in k1, p1 rib for 0.5 (0.5, 1, 1, 1)". BO.

Rep for second armhole edging.

Sew side seams, from hem to underarm, including ribbing.

neck

Using smaller circular needle or dpns and MC, attach yarn at right back neck and k across the 23 (25, 27, 29, 31) sts held for back neck, pick up and knit 24 (26, 28, 30, 32) sts down left side of neck, knit the held center neck st and mark it, pick up and knit 24 (26, 28, 30, 32) sts up right side of neck. 72 (78, 84, 90, 96) sts. Begin working in the round.

Round 1: *P1, k1, rep from * to end of round.

Round 2: Work in rib to 1 st before marked center st, s2kp, work sts as they appear to end of round.

Rep last round 2 (4, 4, 4, 4) more times.

BO in rib.

MATILDA

swing top

by julie turjoman

For twirling and dancing at the water's edge, nothing beats a softly draping fabric like this blend of bamboo and pearl viscose. And in the heat of a summer day, a sleeveless tunic is utterly perfect, especially when it has a pocket for stashing little treasures picked up on the beach. Both the yarn and the resin buttons are machine-washable, making this an easy-care project for busy parents.

directions

back

CO 55 (61, 66, 72, 76) sts.

Next row (RS): Purl.

Work 3 more rows in rev St st for rolled hem.

Next row (RS): Change to St st and work even until piece measures 8 (9.5, 11, 12.5, 12.5)" from CO edge, ending with a WS row.

Shape Armholes

Dec Row (RS): K2, skp, k to last 4 sts, k2tog, k2.

Rep the Dec Row every RS row 2 (2, 3, 4, 5) times. 49 (55, 58, 62, 64) sts.

Work even until Back measures 3.5 (4.5, 5, 5, 5.5)" from beg of armhole shaping.

Shape Shoulders

BO 0 (0, 1, 1, 1) st(s) at beg of next 2 rows.

BO 1 (1, 0, 0, 1) st(s) at beg of next 2 rows.

SIZE

2 (4, 6, 8, 10)

FINISHED MEASUREMENTS

Chest at underarm: 22 (24, 26, 28.5, 30)"

Length: 12 (14, 16, 17, 18)"

MATERIALS

- Sublime *Bamboo & Pearls DK* (70% bamboo-sourced viscose, 30% pearl-sourced viscose; 104 yd. per 50g ball); color: 212 Saffron; 4 (5, 5, 6, 7) balls

- US 5 (3.75mm) needles *(or size needed to match gauge)*

- Size F (3.75mm) crochet hook

- Tapestry needle

- 2 decorative buttons, 1" or larger

continued ➤

➤ continued

GAUGE
22 sts × 34 rows = 4" in St st, blocked

SKILLS USED
Basic decreasing, three-needle bind-off, basic crochet

BO 0 (0, 0, 1, 1) st(s) at beg of next 2 rows.

BO rem 47 (53, 56, 58, 58) sts for back neck.

front

Work as for Back through armhole shaping.

Then work even until the front measures 2.5 (2.5, 3, 3.5, 3.5)" from beg of armhole shaping, ending with a WS row, then shape the neckline.

Shape Neckline
You will work both sides of neck simultaneously using two balls of yarn.

Next row (RS): K17 (19, 19, 21, 21); join new ball of yarn and BO center 15 (17, 20, 20, 22) sts; k to end of row.

Next row (WS): Purl.

Next row (RS): K to 4 sts before neck edge, k2tog, k2; on right side of neck, k2, skp, k to end of row.

Rep the last 2 rows 6 (7, 7, 8, 8) more times. 10 (11, 11, 12, 12) sts rem for each shoulder. Work even until piece measures 12 (14, 16, 17, 18)" or same as Back.

BO rem sts.

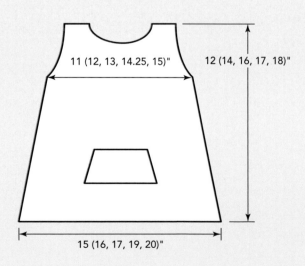

11 (12, 13, 14.25, 15)"

12 (14, 16, 17, 18)"

15 (16, 17, 19, 20)"

side panels

(make 2)

CO 28 (28, 28, 32, 32) sts and work 4 rows in rev St st as for Body, beg with a purl row.

Next row (RS): Change to St st and work even until piece measures 2 (2, 2, 2.5, 2.5)" from CO edge.

Next row (RS): K2, skp, k2, skp, k to last 8 sts, k2tog, k2, k2tog, k2.

Work 7 rows even.

Rep these 8 rows 3 more times.
12 (12, 12, 16, 16) sts rem.

Next row (RS): K2, skp, k to last 4 sts, k2tog, k2.

Work 7 rows even.

Rep these 8 rows twice more. 6 (6, 6, 10, 10) sts.

Work even if necessary until piece measures 8 (9.5, 11, 12.5, 12.5)" from CO edge.

BO rem 6 (6, 6, 10, 10) sts.

pocket

(make 1)

CO 34 (36, 38, 40, 40) sts.

Next row (RS): Knit.

Next row (WS): K3, p28 (30, 32, 34, 34), k3.

Rep these 2 rows until piece measures 2 (2, 2.5, 3, 3)".

Shape Pocket

Next row (RS): *K4, skp, k to last 6 sts, k2tog, k4.

Work 3 rows even maintaining 3 edge sts on both sides in garter st.

Rep these 4 rows 4 (4, 4, 5, 5) more times. 24 (26, 28, 28, 28) sts rem.

Work even until pocket measures 3.5 (4, 4, 4.5, 4.5)".

BO rem sts.

finishing

Weave in all ends. Lightly block all pieces. Stitch the cast-on and bound-off edges of the pocket to the center of the front panel. Stitch up each side of the pocket from the cast-on edge to beg of shaping. Seam side panels to front and back, matching armholes and hem edges. Sew shoulder seams. Work one row of single crochet (see the "Special Knitting Techniques" appendix) around armholes and neck edge. Sew one decorative button at the base of each opening on the pocket.

SHORT SLEEVES

VASHTI
hooded top
with eyelets

VASHTI
hooded top with eyelets

by talitha kuomi

With pockets just big enough for a new favorite rock or small change for penny candy at the corner store, this top takes me back to summer vacations as a child. It evokes fond memories of playing with my cousins on the beach from sunup to sundown, when we donned our hoods against the early evening breeze with hopes that our parents would allow us to stay out just a little while longer.

pattern notes

This pattern is knit from the top down. The hood is knit flat, then you move onto the shoulders. At the bottom of the V-neck, you begin knitting in the round down to the eyelet hem. The pockets are knit separately and sewn on last. For M1L, M1R, RLI, and LLI increase techniques, as well as k3tog, please refer to the "Special Knitting Techniques" appendix.

directions
hood and shoulders

With circular needle, CO 63 (67, 73, 77, 81, 85) sts. Do not join.

Row 1 (RS): Knit.

Row 2: Purl.

Row 3: K30 (31, 33, 34, 35, 36), M1L, place marker (pm), k3 (5, 7, 9, 11, 13), pm, M1R, k to end. 65 (69, 75, 79, 83, 87) sts.

Row 4: Purl.

Row 5: K to last st before m, M1L, k1, slip marker (sm), k to marker, sm, k1, M1R, k to end.

Rep last 2 rows 4 more times. 75 (79, 85, 89, 93, 97) sts.

SIZE
2 (4, 6, 8, 10, 12)

FINISHED MEASUREMENTS
Chest circumference:
22 (24, 26, 27.5, 29, 31)"
Length: 13 (15, 17, 19, 21, 23)"

MATERIALS
- Hemp for Knitting *allhemp6LUX* (100% hemp; 143 yd. per 100g skein); color: 062 Aioli; 3 (4, 5, 5, 5, 6) skeins
- US 6 (4mm) circular needle, 29" length; smaller sizes may need to use 24" length (*or size needed to match gauge*)

continued ➤

➤ continued

- US 7 (4.5mm) double-pointed needles

  US 7 (4.5mm) circular needle, 24" length (optional)

- 5 stitch markers, 1 contrasting
- Tapestry needle
- Stitch holder or scrap yarn

GAUGE
18 sts × 26 rows = 4" in St st, unblocked

SKILLS USED
Basic increasing and decreasing, knitting in the round, eyelets, mattress stitch for hood seam

Continue even in St st until piece measures 4.5 (5, 5.5, 6, 6.5, 7)" from CO row, ending with a WS row.

Decrease for Base of Hood

Next row (RS): K to last 2 sts before m, ssk, sm, k to marker, sm, k2tog, k to end.

Work 5 rows in St st, beg and ending with a purl row.

Rep these 6 rows 6 more times. 61 (65, 71, 75, 79, 83) sts.

Shape Shoulders

Set-up Row (RS): K6 (7, 8, 8, 9, 9), *M1L, k1, pm, k1, M1R*, k10 (11, 12, 13, 13, 14), rep from * to *, k21 (21, 23, 25, 27, 29), removing 2 original markers as you come to them, rep * to *, k10 (11, 12, 13, 13, 14), rep from * to *, k6 (7, 8, 8, 9, 9). 69 (73, 79, 83, 87, 91) sts.

Purl 1 row.

Row 1 (RS): K2, RLI, [k to 1 st before m, M1L, k1, sm, k1, M1R] 4 times, k to last 2 sts, LLI, k2.

Row 2 (WS): Purl.

Row 3: [K to 1 st before m, M1L, k1, sm, k1, M1R] 4 times, k to end.

Row 4: Purl.

Rep these 4 rows 2 (3, 4, 5, 6, 7) more times. 123 (145, 169, 191, 213, 235) sts.

body

You will now join the body in the round.

Next row (RS): [K to last st before m, *M1L, k1, sm, k1, M1R] 4 times, k to end, remove marker and continue knitting to last 2 sts before next marker, and place new beg of round marker. 131 (153, 177, 199, 221, 243) sts.

Round 1: Knit.

Round 2: [K to last st before m, M1L, k1, sm, k1, M1R] 4 times, k to end.

Rep these 2 rounds 7 (6, 5, 4, 3, 2) more times. 195 (209, 225, 239, 253, 267) sts.

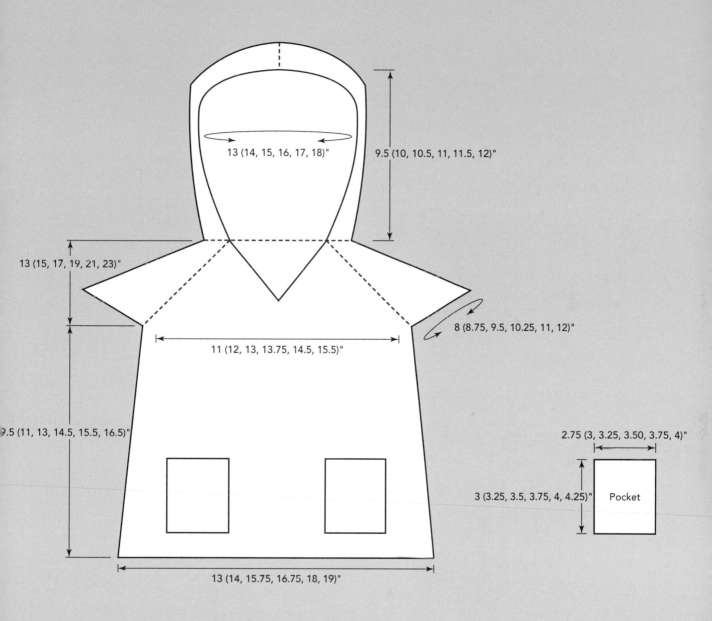

13 (14, 15, 16, 17, 18)"

9.5 (10, 10.5, 11, 11.5, 12)"

13 (15, 17, 19, 21, 23)"

8 (8.75, 9.5, 10.25, 11, 12)"

11 (12, 13, 13.75, 14.5, 15.5)"

9.5 (11, 13, 14.5, 15.5, 16.5)"

2.75 (3, 3.25, 3.50, 3.75, 4)"

3 (3.25, 3.5, 3.75, 4, 4.25)"   Pocket

13 (14, 15.75, 16.75, 18, 19)"

Divide Sleeves and Body

Next round: *K to m, sm, place 44 (47, 50, 53, 55, 58) sts between markers onto holder or scrap yarn, remove marker, rep from *, k to end of round. 107 (115, 125, 133, 143, 151) sts on the needles.

Begin A-line Shaping

Next round: [K to last st before m, M1L, k1, sm, k1, M1R] twice, k to end of round.

Knit 8 (9, 10, 12, 13, 14) rounds even.

Rep these 9 (10, 11, 13, 14, 15) rounds 6 more times. 135 (143, 153, 161, 171, 179) sts.

Continue in St st until piece measures 10 (11, 12, 14, 15, 16)" from where you separated the sleeve sts from the body sts.

Next round: *M1 (1, 1, 0, 1, 1) st, k27 (35, 152, 161, 42, 59) sts slipping the marker when you come to it, rep from * to last 0 (3, 1, 0, 3, 2) st(s), k to end. 140 (147, 154, 161, 175, 182) sts.

Create Eyelet Hem

Remove beg of round marker, k to next marker, this now indicates the new beg of round.

Knit following 4 rounds loosely, going up 1 needle size if desired.

Round 1: *K2tog, yo, skp, k3, rep from * to end.

Round 2: *K1, [p1, k1, p1] in the yo, k1, k3tog, rep from * to end.

Round 3: Knit, removing markers.

Round 4: BO loosely.

sleeves

Transfer 44 (47, 50, 53, 55, 58) sts held for one sleeve onto dpns, pm for beg of round.

Round 1: K1 (3, 1, 2, 4, 1), *k2tog, yo, skp, k3, rep from * to last 1 (2, 0, 2, 2, 1) st(s), k1 (2, 0, 2, 2, 1).

Round 2: K1 (3, 1, 2, 4, 1), *k1, [p1, k1, p1] in the yo, k1, k3tog, rep from * to last 1 (2, 0, 2, 2, 1) st(s), k1 (2, 0, 2, 2, 1).

Round 3: K to end, remove marker.

Round 4: BO loosely.

Rep for second sleeve.

pockets

(make 2)

Using dpns, CO 15 (17, 17, 18, 20, 20) sts.

Work in St st for 2.5 (2.75, 3, 3.25, 3.5, 3.75)", ending on a WS row.

Row 1 (RS): K2 (3, 3, 0, 1, 1), [k2tog, yo, skp, k3] 1 (1, 1, 2, 2, 2) time(s), [k2tog, yo, skp], k2 (3, 3, 0, 1, 1).

Row 2 (WS): P2 (3, 3, 0, 1, 1), *p1, [k1, p1, k1] in the yo, p1, p3tog, rep from * 0 (0, 0, 1, 1, 1) more time(s), p1, [k1, p1, k1] in the yo, p3 (4, 4, 1, 2, 2).

Row 3: Knit.

Row 4: BO purlwise.

finishing

Block pieces. Fold the hood in half and mattress stitch the top edges together. Sew the gaps under the armholes closed. Sew the patch pockets to the lower front of the top. Weave in all ends.

MADELINE
lace panel t-shirt

by susan robicheau

This feminine top features lace panels on the front and sleeves and is sure to make your girl feel pretty. And the snuggly soft yarn is easy care, so she can wear it as often as she likes.

SIZE
6 (8, 10, 12)

FINISHED MEASUREMENTS
Chest circumference: 27 (28.5, 30, 32)"
Length: 14.5 (15.5, 16, 17.25)"

MATERIALS
- Naturally Caron *Spa* (75% acrylic, 25% rayon from bamboo; 251 yd. per 85g skein); color: 0002 Coral Lipstick; 2 (2, 3, 3) skeins
- US 7 (4.5mm) needles, straight or circular *(or size needed to match gauge)*
- US 7 (4.5mm) double-pointed needles or 16" circular for collar
- Stitch markers
- Stitch holders or scrap yarn
- Tapestry needle

GAUGE
20 sts × 24 rows = 4" in St st, unblocked

SKILLS USED
Increasing and decreasing, lace knitting, picking up stitches

pattern notes
The chart in this pattern is available for download at **www.wiley.com/go/moreknittinginthesun.**

seed stitch edging (worked flat)
(worked over an odd number of sts)
Rows 1 and 2: *K1, p1, rep from * to last st, k1.

seed stitch edging (in the round)
(worked over an even number of sts)
Row 1: *K1, p1, rep from * around.
Row 2: *P1, k1, rep from * around.
Rep these 2 rows for Seed st.

lace pattern
(worked over a multiple of 12 sts + 1)
Row 1 and all WS rows: Purl.
Row 2: K1, *k1, [k2tog, yo] twice, k1, [yo, ssk] twice, k2, rep from *.
Row 4: K1, *[k2tog, yo] twice, k3, [yo, ssk] twice, k1, rep from *.

Row 6: K2tog, *yo, k2tog, yo, k5, yo, ssk, yo, sk2p, rep from * ending last rep with ssk.

Row 8: K1, *[yo, ssk] twice, k3, [k2tog, yo] twice, k1, rep from *.

Row 10: K1, *k1, [yo, ssk] twice, k1, [k2tog, yo] twice, k2, rep from *.

Row 12: K1, * k2, yo, ssk, yo, sk2p, yo, k2tog, yo, k3, rep from *.

directions

back

CO 67 (71, 75, 81) sts.

Work 2 rows of Seed Stitch Edging.

Next row (WS): K1, p to last st, k1.

Next row (RS): Knit.

Rep last 2 rows until back measures 8.5, (9.5, 9.5, 10)", ending with a WS row.

Shape Armholes

BO 3 (3, 4, 4) sts at beg of next 2 rows.

Next row: K2, ssk, k to last 4 sts, k2tog, k2.

Next row: K1, p to last st, k1.

Rep last 2 rows 1 (2, 1, 2) time(s). 57 (59, 63, 67) sts.

Work even until back measures 6 (6, 6.5, 7.5)" from beg of armhole shaping.

Shape Shoulders

BO 7 (7, 8, 9) sts at beg of next 2 rows.

BO 8 (8, 9, 9) sts at beg of next 2 rows. Place 27 (29, 29, 31) rem sts on holder or scrap yarn for back neck.

front

CO 67 (71, 75, 81) sts and work 2 rows of Seed Stitch Edging, beginning with a WS row.

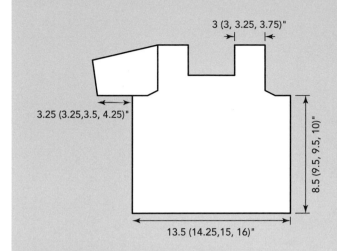

3 (3, 3.25, 3.75)"

3.25 (3.25,3.5, 4.25)"

8.5 (9.5, 9.5, 10)"

13.5 (14.25,15, 16)"

Begin Lace Pattern:

Row 1 (WS): K1, p20 (22, 24, 27), place marker (pm), work 25 sts in Lace Pattern beg with Row 1, pm, p20 (22, 24, 27), k1.

Row 2: K21 (23, 25, 28), work 25 sts in Lace Pattern, k21 (23, 25, 28).

Continue to work in established patt until 51 (57, 57, 61) patt rows completed, or desired length, ending with a WS row.

Shape Armholes

Continue to work Lace Pattern as set while you shape the armholes.

BO 3 (3, 4, 4) sts at beg of next 2 rows.

Next row (RS): K2, ssk, work in patt to last 4 sts, k2tog, k2.

Next row: K1, work in patt to last st, k1.

Rep last 2 rows 1 (2, 1, 2) more time(s). 57 (59, 63, 67) sts.

Work 4 (2, 8, 6) more rows even in patt.

Lace Pattern Chart

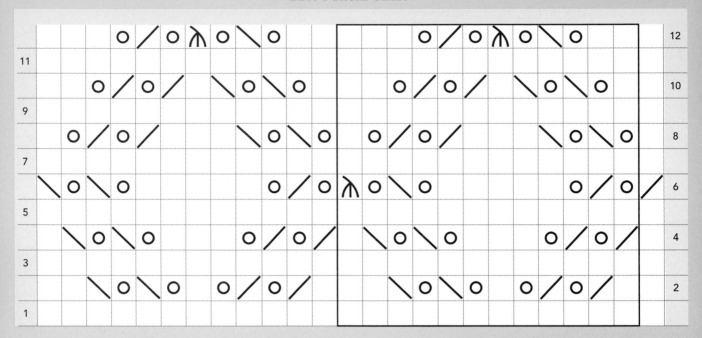

Key to Lace Pattern Chart

knit
RS: knit stitch
WS: purl stitch

k2tog
Knit 2 stitches together as 1 stitch.

yo
Yarn over

ssk
Slip 1 stitch as if to knit, slip another stitch as if to knit.
Insert LH needle into front of these 2 stitches and knit them together.

sk2p
Slip 1, k2tog, pass slipped stitch over k2tog.

Shape Left Neck

Next row (RS): K15 (15, 17, 18) sts, place rem sts on holder (for right neck and shoulder).

Work even on these 15 (15, 17, 18) sts for 25 (25, 25, 29) rows more.

Shape Left Shoulder

Next row (RS): BO 7 (7, 8, 9) sts, k to end.

Next row: K1, p to last st, k1.

Next row: BO 8 (8, 9, 9) rem sts.

Shape Right Neck

Move 15 (15, 17, 18) sts for right neck and shoulder from holder to working needle. Leave center 27 (29, 29, 31) sts on holder for front neck.

Rejoin yarn at neck edge with RS facing. Work even on these 15 (15, 17, 18) sts for 25 (25, 25, 29) rows more, ending with a RS row.

Shape Right Shoulder

Next row (WS): BO 7 (7, 8, 9) sts, p to end.

Next row: Knit.

Next row: BO 8 (8, 9, 9) rem sts.

sleeves

(make 2)

CO 45 (45, 49, 51) sts and work 2 rows of Seed Stitch Edging.

Begin Lace Pattern:

NOTE End Row 6 of Lace Pattern with ssk instead of sk2p.

Row 1 (WS): K1, p15 (15, 17, 18), pm, work 13 sts in Lace Pattern beg with Row 1, pm, p15 (15, 17, 18), k1.

Row 2 (RS): K16 (16, 18, 19), work 13 sts in Lace Pattern, k16 (16, 18, 19).

Continue to work in established patt, increasing 1 st at each end of needle every 6th (6th, 7th, 8th) row twice. 49 (49, 53, 55) sts.

Work even until 19 (19, 21, 25) Lace Pattern rows completed, ending with WS row.

BO 3 (3, 4, 4) sts at beg of next 2 rows.

Dec 1 st at each end of needle every row 5 (3, 0, 0) times.

Dec 1 st at each end of every RS row 9 (11, 14, 14) times.

BO rem 15 (15, 17, 19) sts on next RS row.

finishing

Sew shoulder seams.

neckband

With circular needle or dpns, join yarn at back right neck and knit 27 (29, 29, 31) sts from back neck stitch holder, pm, pick up and knit 23 (23, 25, 27) sts from left front neck edge, pm, knit 27 (29, 29, 31) sts from front neck stitch holder, pm, and pick up and knit 23 (23, 25, 27) sts from right front neck edge, pm. Join sts to beg working in the round. 100 (104, 108, 116) sts.

Round 1: *K1, p1, rep from * around.

Round 2: *Ssk, work seed st to 2 sts before marker, k2tog, sm, p2tog-tbl, seed st to 2 sts before marker, p2tog, sm, rep from * once. 8 sts dec'd.

Round 3: Rep Round 2.

BO in patt, working decreases as set at each marker as you do.

Sew sleeves in place. Sew side seams. Weave in ends. Block.

MAX
striped baseball t-shirt

MAX
striped baseball t-shirt

by kate oates

This pocket tee is perfect for warmer weather and playtime. Cotton fiber makes it both breathable and machine washable. The top features sweet stripes suitable for any age, and seamless construction means that when you're done knitting, you're done with the project.

pattern notes

This tee is worked from the bottom up in the round with raglan-style decreases. The sleeves are worked in the round and attached seamlessly. The pattern contains instructions for intarsia in the round for colorwork. The pocket is knit separately and sewn on. For M1L and M1R increases, as well as grafting instructions, please refer to the "Special Knitting Techniques" appendix.

decreases

Sssk: Sl 3 sts knitwise, one at a time, insert LH needle into fronts of these sts from left to right and knit them together.

Sssp: Wyif, sl 3 sts knitwise, one at a time, sl these sts back to LH needle and purl the 3 sts tog tbl.

directions
body

Using MC and longer circular needle, CO 102 (112, 120, 128, 136, 144) sts. Place marker (pm) and join to knit in the round, being careful not to twist sts.

Knit 1" in St st with MC. (Edge will roll.)

SIZE
2 (4, 6, 8, 10, 12)

FINISHED MEASUREMENTS
Chest circumference: 22.75 (25, 26.75, 28.5, 30.25, 32)"
Length: 12.5 (14, 14.5, 15.5, 16.5, 17.5)"

MATERIALS
- Rowan *Handknit Cotton* (100% cotton; 92 yd. per 50g skein); [MC] color: 239 Ice Water, 2 (3, 3, 4, 4, 4) skeins; [CC] color: 335 Thunder, 1 (2, 2, 2, 3, 3) skein(s)
- US 7 (4.5mm) circular needle, 24" length (*or size needed to match gauge*)

continued ➤

➤ **continued**

- US 7 (4.5mm) circular needle, 16" length
- US 7 (4.5mm) double-pointed needles
- Tapestry needle
- Stitch markers
- Bobbins for intarsia (optional)

GAUGE

18 sts × 23 rows = 4" in St st, blocked

SKILLS USED

Basic increasing and decreasing, following multiple sets of instructions at the same time, intarsia in the round, picking up stitches, grafting

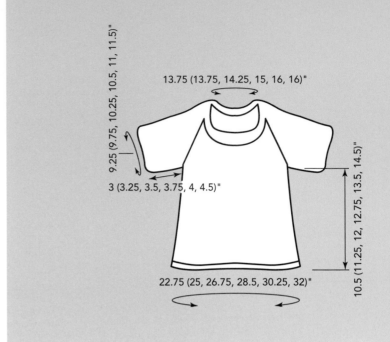

Begin Stripe Pattern as follows:

Rounds 1 and 2: Knit in CC.

Rounds 3 and 4: Knit in MC.

Rep these 4 rounds until piece measures 10.5 (11, 12, 12.5, 13.5, 14.5)" from CO edge, ending after Round 4 of Stripe Pattern. Set aside.

sleeves

(make 2)

Using MC and dpns, CO 34 (36, 38, 40, 42, 44) sts. Pm and join in the round, being careful not to twist sts.

Work even in St st for 1" with MC.

Inc Round: K1, M1L, k to last st, M1R, k1.

Rep Inc Round every 4th round 3 more times. 42 (44, 46, 48, 50, 52) sts.

Work even in St st until sleeve measures 3 (3.25, 3.5, 3.75, 4, 4.5)" from CO edge.

Next round: K to last 4 (4, 5, 5, 5, 6) sts; sl 8 (8, 10, 10, 10, 12) sts to st holder or scrap yarn for underarm, removing end of round marker as you pass it; set rem 34 (36, 36, 38, 40, 40) sts aside.

Join Sleeves to Body

Return to needle holding body sts. With MC, k18 (20, 21, 22, 24, 25) for right front, slip next 8 (8, 10, 10, 10, 12) sts to holder or scrap yarn for underarm, pm, k34 (36, 36, 38, 40, 40) sts from first sleeve (with underarm sts of sleeve and body aligned), pm, k43 (48, 50, 54, 58, 60) sts for back, slip next 8 (8, 10, 10, 10, 12) sts to holder or scrap yarn, pm, k34 (36, 36, 38, 40, 40) sts from second sleeve, pm, k25 (28, 29, 32, 34, 35) sts for left front. 154 (168, 172, 184, 196, 200) sts.

Knit 1 round with MC.

yoke

The yoke is worked in an intarsia method that allows you to work in the round and maintain stripes over the front and back while keeping the sleeves in MC only. You will turn the work and purl on Round 2 to do so. You will need 2 balls of MC and 3 balls of CC; bobbins or small balls of yarn can be used.

You will decrease every odd-numbered round. Remember that you will switch colors at the markers on Round 1 as you decrease. Read through this section to familiarize yourself with the technique before beginning.

Round 1 (Dec Round): Switch to CC and work across right front to 3 sts before marker, k2tog, k1, sm; with ball of MC: k1, ssk, work across first sleeve to 3 sts before marker, k2tog, k1, sm; with ball of CC: k1, ssk, work across back to 3 sts before marker, k2tog, k1, sm; with ball of MC: k1, ssk, work across second sleeve to 3 sts before marker, k2tog, k1, sm; with ball of CC: k1, ssk, work across left front; wyib sl next st purlwise onto RH needle; move yarn to front then sl st back onto LH needle. Turn.

Round 2: Purl to wrapped st, switching colors at markers. Pick up wrap: insert RH needle through wrap and through st purlwise, purl st, lift wrap off over new st to front. Wrap next st as follows: Sl 1 st purlwise. Move yarn to back and turn work so knit side is facing. Sl the same st to RH needle purlwise and move yarn to back once more.

Round 3 (Dec Round): Switch to MC and work all the way around without changing balls of yarn, decreasing as follows: *K to 3 sts before marker, k2tog, k1, sm, k1, ssk; rep from * 3 more times, k to end of round. Insert RH needle through wrap and through st knitwise. Knit st, lift wrap off over new st to back.

Round 4: Knit in MC.

Work these 4 rounds a total of 4 (5, 5, 5, 6, 7) times. 90 (88, 92, 104, 100, 88) sts.

neckline

NOTE For this section, the piece is worked back and forth instead of in the round. Continue working intarsia stripes, but wrapping & turning is no longer necessary. Purl all WS rows.

Next row (RS): K1, ssk, *k to 3 sts before marker, k2tog, k1, sm, k1, ssk, rep from * 3 times, k7 (7, 8, 9, 9, 8), k2tog, k1.

Sl rem 7 (8, 8, 10, 10, 10) sts to holder or scrap yarn for front neck; turn.

Next RS row (Dec Row): K1, ssk, *k to 3 sts before marker, k2tog, k1, sm, k1, ssk, rep from * 3 times, k to last 3 sts, k2tog, k1.

Rep Dec Row every RS row 0 [0, 1, 1, 1, 0] more time(s). 63 (60, 54, 64, 60, 58) sts.

Purl 1 row.

Next row (Neck Shaping Row) (RS): *K to 3 sts before marker, k2tog, k1, sm, k1, ssk, rep from * 3 times.

Rep Neck Shaping Row every RS row 2 [2, 1, 2, 1, 1] more time(s). 34 (36, 38, 40, 44, 42) sts.

Remove markers on final WS row.

collar

Work collar in MC using 16" circular needle or dpns. K across 34 (36, 38, 40, 44, 42) sts on needle; pick up and knit 7 (7, 8, 8, 9, 10) sts along left front collar; knit across the 7 (8, 8, 10, 10, 10) sts held for front neck; pick up and knit 7 (7, 8, 8, 9, 10) sts along right front collar. Place marker and join to work in the round. 55 (58, 62, 66, 72, 72) sts.

Knit in the round for 1". BO loosely.

pocket

Using MC, CO 13 (13, 13, 17, 17, 17) sts, leaving a long tail for sewing.

Work back and forth in St st until piece measures 2.5 (2.5, 2.5, 3, 3, 3)" from CO edge, ending on a WS row.

Dec on the next 2 (2, 2, 3, 3, 3) rows as follows:

RS Dec Row: K1, sssk, k to last 3 sts, k3tog, k1.

WS Dec Row: P1, p3tog, p to last 3 sts, sssp, p1.

5 sts rem.

Next Row: Sssk, k2tog, pass first st over second st. Cut yarn and pull through rem st to secure.

finishing

Using pocket's long tail from the cast-on, sew pocket to left front of sweater. Make sure you do not sew the top closed, and allow the top of the pocket to roll slightly before sewing it down. Graft underarms closed with kitchener stitch. Weave in all loose ends. Block if desired.

THUMBELINA
cap-sleeved top

THUMBELINA
cap-sleeved top

by katya frankel

This sweetly feminine top is perfect for your little princess without being too fussy for everyday wear. An eyelet pattern adds subtle interest to the hemline while smart neck and armhole shaping give it a perfect fit. The overlapping petals on the cap sleeves are worked with short rows.

pattern notes

For w&t and three-needle bind-off, please refer to the "Special Knitting Techniques" appendix.

decreases

Ssp: Sl 2 sts knitwise, one at a time, return them to LH needle, insert RH needle into backs of these 2 sts and p2tog.

eyelet pattern

(worked over a multiple of 6 sts + 2)

Rows 1–4: Work in St st.

Row 5 (RS): K1, p to last st, k1.

Row 6 (WS): P1, *k2, p2tog, yo, k2; rep from * to last st, p1.

Rows 7 and 8: Work in St st.

Rep these 8 rows for patt.

directions

This top is knit in pieces from the bottom up; sleeves are shaped with short rows.

back

With straight needles, CO 66 (74, 78, 86, 90) sts and begin ribbing as follows:

SIZE
2 (4, 6, 8, 10)

FINISHED MEASUREMENTS
Chest circumference:
22 (24.5, 26, 28.5, 30)"
Length: 13.25 (14.75, 16.5, 19.25, 20.75)"

MATERIALS
- Rowan *Pima Cotton DK* (100% pima cotton; 142 yd. per 50g ball); color: 56 Icing; 3 (3, 4, 4, 4) balls
- US 4 (3.5mm) straight needles (*or size needed to match gauge*)
- US 4 (3.5mm) double-pointed needles or 16" circular

continued ➤

Next row (WS): *P2, k2; rep from * to last 2 sts, p2.

Work sts as they appear for 2 more rows.

Work 3 rep of the 8-row Eyelet Pattern.

Switch to St st and work even until body measures 8.75 (9.75, 11, 13, 14)", ending with a WS row.

Shape Armholes

BO 3 (4, 4, 5, 5) sts at beg of next 2 rows. 60 (66, 70, 76, 80) sts.

BO 2 sts at beg of next 2 rows. 56 (62, 66, 72, 76) sts.

Next row (RS): K1, k2tog, k to last 3 sts, ssk, k1.

Next row (WS): Purl.

Rep last 2 rows 2 (3, 4, 5, 6) more times. 50 (54, 56, 60, 62) sts.

Work 22 (24, 26, 28, 30) rows even ending with WS row.

Shape Back Neck and Shoulders

Begin with right shoulder only.

Next row (RS): K17 (18, 19, 20, 21), slip rem sts to stitch holder or scrap yarn if desired, turn.

Next row (WS): BO 2 sts, p to last 4 (4, 5, 5, 5) sts, w&t.

Next row (RS): Knit.

Next row (WS): BO 2 sts, p to last 8 (8, 9, 10, 10) sts, w&t.

Next row (RS): Knit.

Next row (WS): BO 2 sts, p across the 11 (12, 13, 14, 15) shoulder sts, picking up wraps and purling them tog with wrapped sts, then place these sts on holder or scrap yarn.

Place 16 (18, 18, 20, 20) center sts on holder or scrap yarn for back neck.

With WS facing, rejoin yarn at outside edge to work left shoulder.

Next row (WS): P17 (18, 19, 20, 21), turn.

Next row (RS): BO 2 sts, k to last 4 (4, 5, 5, 5) sts, w&t.

Next row (WS): Purl.

Next row (RS): BO 2 sts, k to last 8 (8, 9, 10, 10) sts, w&t.

Next row (WS): Purl.

Next row (RS): BO 2 sts, k across the 11 (12, 13, 14, 15) shoulder sts, picking up wraps and knitting them tog with wrapped sts, then place these sts on holder or scrap yarn.

➤ continued

- 2 stitch markers
- Tapestry needle
- Straight pins
- Stitch holders or scrap yarn

GAUGE
24 sts × 30 rows = 4" in St st, unblocked

SKILLS USED
Basic increases and decreases, short rows (w&t), three-needle bind-off, picking up stitches

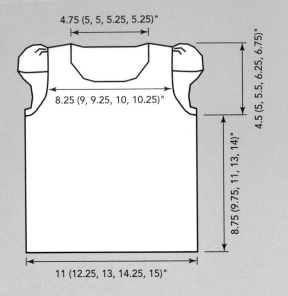

4.75 (5, 5, 5.25, 5.25)"

8.25 (9, 9.25, 10, 10.25)"

4.5 (5, 5.5, 6.25, 6.75)"

8.75 (9.75, 11, 13, 14)"

11 (12.25, 13, 14.25, 15)"

front

Work as for Back until armhole shaping.

Shape Armholes
BO 3 (4, 4, 5, 5) sts at beg of next 2 rows.
60 (66, 70, 76, 80) sts.

BO 2 sts at beg of next 2 rows. 56 (62, 66, 72, 76) sts.

Next row (RS): K1, k2tog, k to last 3 sts, ssk, k1.

Next row (WS): Purl.

Rep last 2 rows 2 (3, 4, 5, 6) more times.
50 (54, 56, 60, 62) sts.

Work 4 (4, 6, 8, 10) rows even ending with WS row.

Shape Left Neck and Shoulder
Begin with left side of neck only.

Next row (RS): K20 (22, 23, 25, 26), turn.

Next row (WS): BO 3 sts, p to end.

Next row (RS): K17 (19, 20, 22, 23).

Next row (WS): BO 2 sts, p to end.

Next row (RS): K15 (17, 18, 20, 21).

Next row (WS): P1, ssp, p to end.

Next row (RS): Knit.

Rep last 2 rows 3 (4, 4, 5, 5) times;
11 (12, 13, 14, 15) sts rem.

Work even until armhole measures same as back armhole to beg of shoulder shaping, ending with RS row.

Next row (WS): P to last 4 (4, 5, 5, 5) sts, w&t.

Next row (RS): Knit.

Next row (WS): P to last 8 (8, 9, 10, 10) sts, w&t.

Next row (RS): Knit.

Next row (WS): P across all 11 (12, 13, 14, 15) shoulder sts, picking up wraps and purling them tog with wrapped sts.

Place left shoulder sts on holder or scrap yarn.

Shape Right Neck and Shoulder
With WS facing, rejoin yarn at outside edge.

Next row (WS): P20 (22, 23, 25, 26), turn. Place 10 rem unworked sts on holder for center neck.

Next row (RS): BO 3 sts, k to end.

Next row (WS): P17 (19, 20, 22, 23).

Next row (RS): BO 2 sts, k to end.

Next row (WS): P15 (17, 18, 20, 21).

Next row (RS): K1, k2tog, k to end.

Next row (WS): Purl.

Rep last 2 rows 3 (4, 4, 5, 5) times; 11 (12, 13, 14, 15) sts rem.

Work even until armhole measures same as back armhole to beg of shoulder shaping, ending with WS row.

Next row (RS): K to last 4 (4, 5, 5, 5) sts, w&t.

Next row (WS): Purl.

Next row (RS): K to last 8 (8, 9, 10, 10) sts, w&t.

Next row (WS): Purl.

Next row (RS): Knit across all shoulder sts, picking up wraps and knitting them tog with wrapped sts.

Join Shoulders

Transfer right back and right front shoulder sts to dpns. Hold pieces with RS together, and working from shoulder edge toward neck, join shoulders with three-needle bind-off. Join the left shoulder the same way.

sleeves

(make 2)

The construction of the sleeve is unusual, and it will not resemble a conventional sleeve as you are knitting it. When the sleeve is complete you will have a curved petal shape at each end connected by a short band. The two petals are overlapped and sewn in place, and the thin section in the middle becomes the underarm.

With straight needle, CO 86 (90, 94, 102, 110) sts.

Starting with WS row, work in 2 × 2 rib for 3 rows.

First Petal

Row 1 (RS): K34 (35, 36, 38, 40), w&t.

Row 2 (WS): Purl.

Row 3: K to 1 st before wrapped st, w&t.

Row 4: Purl.

Row 5: K1, k2tog, knit to 1 st before wrapped st, w&t.

Rep Rows 2–5 once more, then rep last 2 rows (Rows 4 & 5) 3 (4, 5, 5, 6) more times.

Next row: Purl.

Next row: [K1, k2tog] 9 (7, 5, 3, 3) times, k across all sts on needle. 72 (77, 82, 92, 99) sts.

Second Petal

Row 1: P34 (35, 36, 38, 40), w&t.

Row 2: Knit.

Row 3: P to 1 st before wrapped st, w&t.

Row 4: Knit to last 3 sts, ssk, k1.

Row 5: P to 1 st before wrapped st, w&t.

Rep Rows 2–5 once more, then rep last 2 rows (Rows 4 & 5) 3 (4, 5, 5, 6) more times.

Next row: Knit to last 19 (15, 11, 7, 7) sts, ssk 9 (7, 5, 3, 3) times, k1.

Next row: Purl to end.

BO all sts.

finishing

Sew side seams. Fold sleeve in half to find the center and mark it. Overlap the tops of the sleeve, so that first and last bound-off sts are on top of one another and pin them together. Place marked center of sleeve at underarm seam and ease sleeve into place, being sure that the top petal of the sleeve is in front. Beg at ribbed edge of top petal, located midway up the front of the armhole opening, seam the sleeve into place, sewing only the top layer. Work over the shoulder, down the back of the armhole opening, and continue up the front. When you come to the front petal, stitch the underlayer of the sleeve in place on the inside. Rep with second sleeve, being sure that the top petal of the sleeve is to the front.

collar

With dpns or 16" circular needle, join yarn and knit across back neck sts from holder, pick up and knit 21 (22, 24, 25, 25) sts to front neck, knit front neck sts from holder, pick up and knit 21 (22, 24, 25, 25) sts to back neck. 68 (72, 76, 80, 80) sts.

Work 3 rounds in 2 × 2 rib. BO in patt. Weave in all ends. Block piece if desired.

LONG SLEEVES

EDMUND
summer henley

EDMUND
summer henley
by susan robicheau

T his easygoing pullover is just the thing to fend off morning chills or evening breezes. A looser-than-expected gauge keeps it cool and casual, while still looking sharp. Knit to tunic length in a bold color, girls will love to wear this, too!

pattern notes

This pullover is worked flat; the shoulders are attached with three-needle bind-off. The drop shoulder sleeves are sewn in place. Stitches are picked up at the neck to complete the Henley collar and buttonbands.

rib pattern 1

(worked over a multiple of 5 sts + 2)

Row 1 (RS): *K2, p3, rep from * to last 2 sts, k2.

Row 2 (WS): Purl.

Rep these 2 rows for patt.

rib pattern 2

(worked over a multiple of 5 sts + 2)

Row 1 (RS): *P2, k3, rep from * to last 2 sts, p2.

Row 2 (WS): Purl.

Rep these 2 rows for patt.

directions
back

CO 57 (62, 67, 72, 77, 82) sts.

Knit 3 rows.

SIZE

2 (4, 6, 8, 10, 12)

FINISHED MEASUREMENTS

Chest circumference: 23 (25, 27, 28.5, 31, 33)"

Length: 11.75 (12.75, 14.25, 15.5, 17.75, 19.25)"

MATERIALS

- Zitron *Savanna Zitron* (60% cotton, 20% linen, 20% rayon; 110 yd. per 50g ball); color: 19 Wheat; 4 (5, 6, 6, 8, 10) balls

- US 6 (4mm) circular needle, any length (*or size needed to match gauge*)

- Spare needle for three-needle bind-off

continued ➤

➤ **continued**
- Stitch holders or scrap yarn
- 3 (3, 3, 4, 4, 4) buttons, 3/4"
- Tapestry needle
- 2 safety pins or removable stitch markers
- Needle and sewing thread to sew buttons

GAUGE
20 sts × 28 rows = 4" in *both* Rib Patterns

21 sts × 27 rows = 4" in St st, blocked

SKILLS USED
Rib patterns, basic increasing and decreasing, picking up stitches, three-needle bind-off, seaming, sewing on buttons

Work 40 (44, 50, 58, 68, 76) rows in Rib Pattern 1. Piece will measure approx 6 (6.5, 7.5, 8.5, 10, 11)". Work more rows if longer length is desired.

Make rev St st band as follows:

Next row (RS): Purl.

Next row: Knit.

Rep last 2 rows once.

Purl 2 rows.

Work in Rib Pattern 2 for 40 (44, 48, 50, 54, 58) rows. Back now measures 12 (12.75, 14.25, 15.5, 17.5, 19.25)".

Transfer sts to holder or scrap yarn.

front

Work same as for Back through rev St st band.

Left Front
Next row (RS): Work 27 (29, 31, 34, 36, 39) sts in Rib Pattern 2, turn. Place rem 30 (33, 36, 38, 41, 43) sts on holder or scrap yarn.

Continue to work in Rib Pattern 2 until 32 (34, 34, 36, 40, 44) rows are completed above rev St st band.

Next row (RS): Work in patt to last 9 (9, 10, 11, 12, 12) sts, then place these sts on holder or scrap yarn for neck. Turn.

Next row: Purl. 18 (20, 21, 23, 24, 27) sts.

Next row: Work in patt to last 3 sts, k2tog, k1.

Rep last 2 rows 1 (2, 2, 2, 2, 3) more time(s).

Continue in patt until 40 (44, 48, 50, 54, 58) rows in Rib Pattern 2 are completed.

Transfer these 16 (17, 18, 20, 21, 23) sts to holder or scrap yarn for shoulder.

Right Front
Tranfer held sts to working needle and attach yarn at neck opening with RS facing. BO 3 (4, 5, 4, 5, 4) sts and beg Rib Pattern 2 as follows: P0 (0, 1, 0, 1, 0), k0 (2, 3, 2, 3, 2), *p2, k3, rep from * to last 2 sts, p2.

Work in Rib Pattern 2 until 31 (33, 33, 35, 39, 43) rows are completed above rev St st band.

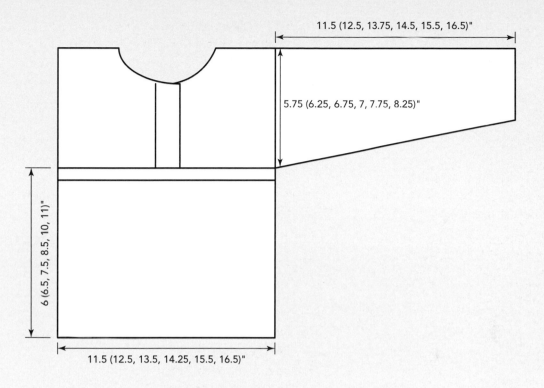

11.5 (12.5, 13.75, 14.5, 15.5, 16.5)"

5.75 (6.25, 6.75, 7, 7.75, 8.25)"

6 (6.5, 7.5, 8.5, 10, 11)"

11.5 (12.5, 13.5, 14.25, 15.5, 16.5)"

Next row (WS): P to last 9 (9, 10, 11, 12, 12) sts, place them on a holder or scrap yarn for neck; turn. 18 (20, 21, 23, 24, 27) sts.

Next row: K1, ssk, work in patt to end of row.

Next row: Purl.

Rep last 2 rows 1 (2, 2, 2, 2, 3) more time(s). 16 (17, 18, 20, 21, 23) sts.

Continue to work in patt until 40 (44, 48, 50, 54, 58) rows of Rib Pattern 2 are completed.

Place sts on holder or scrap yarn.

sleeves

(make 2)

CO 22 (27, 27, 32, 32, 37) sts.

Knit 1 WS row.

Work 8 rows in Rib Pattern 1.

Rev St st band:

Next row (RS): Purl.

Next row: Knit.

Next row: Purl.

Work 3 rows in St st beg with WS row.

Inc Row (RS): K1, kfb, k to last 3 sts, kfb, k2.

Rep Inc Row every RS row 13 (5, 6, 3, 5, 2) times, then every 4th row 4 (12, 13, 16, 17, 20) times. 58 (63, 67, 72, 78, 83) sts.

Continue to work in St st without increasing until sleeve measures 11.5 (12.5, 13.75, 14.5, 15.5, 16.5)".

BO.

finishing

Transfer sts held for back to one needle; transfer sts held for left and right front shoulders to spare needle. With front and back held RS together, use three-needle bind-off (see the "Special Knitting Techniques" appendix) to join 16 (17, 18, 20, 21, 23) shoulder sts, k across 25 (28, 31, 32, 35, 36) back neck sts, use three-needle bind-off to join rem 16 (17, 18, 20, 21, 23) shoulder sts.

With RS facing, beg at bottom of neck placket on right front and pick up and knit 20 (22, 22, 23, 26, 28) sts up side of placket, mark next st with safety pin (or removable st marker), k across 9 (9, 10, 11, 12, 12) sts on holder for right front neck, pick up and knit 5 (6, 9, 9, 9, 9) sts to shoulder, k across 25 (28, 31, 32, 35, 36) sts held for back neck, pick up and knit 5 (6, 9, 9, 9, 9) sts from shoulder to next set of held sts, k 9 (9, 10, 11, 12, 12) sts from holder, mark last st knit with safety pin (or removable st marker), pick up and knit 20 (22, 22, 23, 26, 28) sts down side of placket. 93 (102, 113, 118, 129, 134) sts.

Row 1 (WS): Knit.

Row 2 (RS): K to marked st, m1, k1, m1, k to marked st, m1, k1, m1, k to end of row.

Rep these 2 rows once more.

make buttonholes

Row 5 (WS): K3 (3, 3, 3, 3, 2), yo, k2tog, [k5 (6, 6, 4, 4, 5), yo, k2tog] 2 (2, 2, 3, 3, 3) times, k to end of row.

Row 6: Rep Row 2.

Row 7: Knit.

BO.

Sew neckbands in place at bottom, being sure that buttonholes are on top. Sew sleeves in place between rev St st bands.

Sew side and sleeve seams. Attach buttons opposite buttonholes. Weave in ends.

Block sweater.

LUCY
ruffled top

LUCY
ruffled top

by tabetha hedrick

A dorned with ruffles and a bit of lace, this quick knit makes a sweet top for your charming tot, and big girls will love it, too! The supersoft yarn and easy-to-wear silhouette will make it a favorite any day of the year.

directions

back

CO 90 (97, 106, 116, 120, 130) sts.

Row 1 (WS): [K1, p1] to last st, k1.

Next row (RS): Beg St st and work even for 0.5", ending with a WS row.

Next row (RS): K0 (0, 2, 0, 2, 0), *k5, k2tog, rep from * to last 6 (6, 6, 4, 6, 4) sts, k to end. 78 (84, 92, 100, 104, 112) sts.

Purl 1 row.

Dec Row (RS): K1, ssk, k to last 3 sts, k2tog, k1.

Continue in St st and rep Dec Row every 4th row 0 (0, 1, 2, 2, 3) more time(s). 76 (82, 88, 94, 98, 104) sts.

Continue in St st until back measures 8.25 (9.25, 9.5, 11, 12, 12.5)", ending with a WS row.

Shape Armholes

BO 4 (5, 5, 5, 5, 6) sts at beg of next 2 rows.

Next row (RS): K1, ssk, k to last 3 sts, k2tog, k1.

Next row: Purl.

Rep these 2 rows 4 (4, 4, 5, 5) more times. 58 (62, 68, 74, 76, 80) sts rem.

Work even until armhole measures 4.25 (4.75, 5, 5.5, 6, 6.5)".

continued ➤

SIZE
2 (4, 6, 8, 10, 12)

FINISHED MEASUREMENTS
Chest circumference:
23.5 (25, 27, 29, 30, 32)"
Length: 13 (14.5, 15, 17.25, 18.75, 19.75)"

MATERIALS
- Crystal Palace Yarns *Panda Silk DK* (52% bamboo, 43% superwash merino wool, 5% combed silk; 120 yd. per 50g ball); color: 6006 Berry Smoothie; 4 (4, 4, 5, 5, 5) balls
- US 6 (4mm) straight needles *(or size needed to match gauge)*
- US 6 (4mm) circular needle, 16" length

Shape Shoulders

BO 7 (8, 9, 7, 7, 7) sts at beg of next 2 rows.

BO 8 (9, 10, 8, 8, 8) sts at beg of next 2 rows.

Sizes 8, 10, and 12 only: BO 8 sts at beg of next 2 rows.

Place rem 28 (28, 30, 28, 30, 34) sts for back neckline on a holder or scrap yarn.

front

Work as for Back through armhole shaping.

Work even in St st until armhole measures 2.25 (2.75, 3, 3.5, 4, 4.5)", ending with a WS row.

Shape Front Neck

Next row (RS): K22 (24, 26, 30, 30, 32) sts, place center 14 (14, 16, 14, 16, 16) sts on holder. Join new yarn and k across rem 22 (24, 26, 30, 30, 32) sts.

➤ continued
- Tapestry needle
- Sewing pins

GAUGE
26 sts × 31 rows = 4" in St st, blocked

SKILLS USED
Basic increasing and decreasing, picking up stitches, simple lace

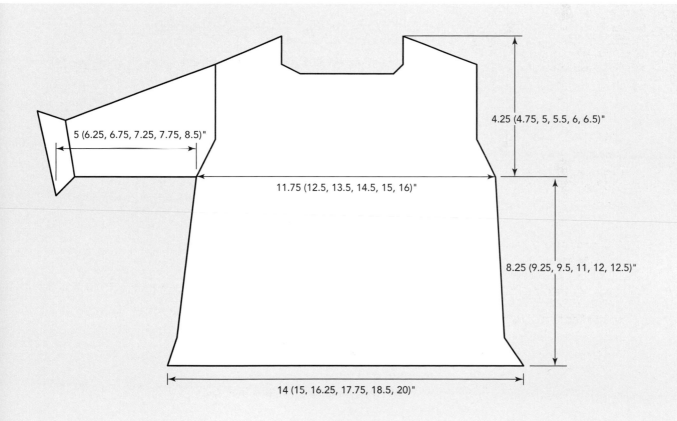

5 (6.25, 6.75, 7.25, 7.75, 8.5)"

4.25 (4.75, 5, 5.5, 6, 6.5)"

11.75 (12.5, 13.5, 14.5, 15, 16)"

8.25 (9.25, 9.5, 11, 12, 12.5)"

14 (15, 16.25, 17.75, 18.5, 20)"

Work both sides of neck as follows:

Next row (RS): On left neck, k to last 3 sts, k2tog, k1; on right neck, k1, ssk, k to end.

Next row: Purl.

Rep these 2 rows 6 (6, 6, 6, 6, 8) more times. 15 (17, 19, 23, 23, 23) sts for each shoulder.

Work even in St st until armholes measure 4.25 (4.75, 5, 5.5, 6, 6.5)".

Shape Shoulders

Next row (RS): BO 7 (8, 9, 7, 7, 7) sts, k to neck; k across right shoulder.

Next row (WS): BO 7 (8, 9, 7, 7, 7) sts, p to neck; p across left shoulder.

Next row (RS): BO 8 (9, 10, 8, 8, 8) sts, k to neck; k across right shoulder.

Next row (WS): BO 8 (9, 10, 8, 8, 8) sts, p to neck; p across left shoulder.

Sizes 8, 10, and 12 only:

Next row (RS): BO 8, k across right shoulder sts.

Next row (WS): BO 8 sts.

sleeves

(make 2)

CO 94 (102, 106, 114, 122, 126) sts. Work in St st for 1.25".

Next row (RS): K1, *k2tog, rep from * to last st, k1. 48 (52, 54, 58, 62, 64) sts.

Knit 2 rows.

Next row (WS): P1, *yo, p2tog; rep from * to last st, p1.

Purl 2 rows.

Work in St st until sleeve measures 5 (6.25, 6.75, 7.25, 7.75, 8.5)" from CO edge, ending with a WS row.

Shape Sleeve Cap

BO 4 (5, 5, 5, 5, 6) sts at beg of next 2 rows.

Dec Row (RS): K1, ssk, k to last 3 sts, k2tog, k1.

Next row (WS): Purl.

Rep these 2 rows 8 (8, 8, 1, 2, 1) time(s).

Then rep Dec Row every 4th row 2 (3, 4, 8, 9, 10) times. 18 (18, 18, 28, 28, 28) sts.

BO 2 (2, 2, 4, 4, 4) sts at beg of next 4 rows.

BO rem 10 (10, 10, 12, 12, 12) sts knitwise on WS row.

finishing

Block pieces to measurements, pinning ruffles into desired placement. Sew shoulders and then sew sleeve caps in place. Sew side and sleeve seams.

With RS facing and circular needle, rejoin yarn and k across 28 (28, 30, 28, 30, 34) sts held for back neck, pick up and knit 12 sts along left neck edge, 14 (14, 16, 14, 16, 16) sts across center front, and 12 sts along right neck edge. 66 (66, 70, 66, 70, 74) sts. Place marker and join for working in the round.

Round 1: Purl.

Round 2: Knit.

Round 3: *Yo, k2tog; rep from * to end of round.

Round 4: Purl.

Round 5: Knit.

BO loosely.

FERN
cropped
pullover

FERN
cropped pullover
by lisa limber

This soft, bulky cotton sweater is the perfect thing to throw on at the beach for an evening bonfire, while playing Scrabble on the porch on a rainy summer day, or for watching fireworks on the Fourth of July. This cropped pullover is perfect to wear with a long T-shirt and jeans in cooler weather, too.

pattern notes

This garment is knit in one piece. The bottom of the sweater is knit in the round. When you begin the top portion of the sweater and the sleeves, you will place half of the stitches from the round onto scrap yarn to work on later. The front and back sections are knit separately from the waist up and then sewn together with the seams on the outside.

staggered rib pattern

(worked in the round)

Rounds 1–3: *K1, p1, rep from * around.

Rounds 4–6: *P1, k1, rep from * around.

directions
body

Using cable cast-on (see the "Special Knitting Techniques" appendix), CO 104 (112, 120, 128, 136) sts.

Join in the round and place marker (pm) to mark beg of round.

Work the 6 rounds of Staggered Rib Pattern 4 (5, 6, 7, 8) times. Piece measures approximately 4.75 (6, 7.25, 8.5, 9.5)".

SIZE
4 (6, 8, 10, 12)

FINISHED MEASUREMENTS
Chest circumference:
30 (32, 34, 36.5, 39)"
Length: 12 (13.5, 15, 16.5, 18)"

MATERIALS
- Punta Yarns *Punta Cotton* (100% cotton; 133 yd. per 100g skein); color: 39; 3 (4, 4, 5, 6) skeins
- US 10 (6mm) circular needle, 24" length *(or size needed to match gauge)*
- 8 stitch markers
- 1 yard of smooth scrap yarn

continued ➤

Slip last 52 (56, 60, 64, 68) sts to scrap yarn and secure; 52 (56, 60, 64, 68) sts on needle for front.

Top Front and Sleeves

You will now work back and forth on the front and cast on for the sleeves.

With RS facing, pm, and, using the cable cast-on method, CO 13 (14, 15, 16, 17) sts, pm, CO another 13 (14, 15, 16, 17) sts.

Continuing on the RS, k13 (14, 15, 16, 17), slip marker (sm), p13 (14, 15, 16, 17), sm, k13 (14, 15, 16, 17), pm, p13 (14, 15, 16, 17), pm, k13 (14, 15, 16, 17), pm, p13 (14, 15, 16, 17), turn.

With WS facing, pm and using the cable cast-on method, CO 13 (14, 15, 16, 17) sts, pm, CO another 13 (14, 15, 16, 17) sts. You will have a total of 104 (112, 120, 128, 136) sts on your needles.

Continuing on WS, k13 (14, 15, 16, 17), sm, p13 (14, 15, 16, 17), sm, k13 (14, 15, 16, 17), sm, p13 (14, 15, 16, 17), sm, k13 (14, 15, 16, 17), sm, p13 (14, 15, 16, 17), turn.

Next row (RS): [K13 (14, 15, 16, 17), sm, p13 (14, 15, 16, 17), sm] 4 times.

Next row (WS): [P13 (14, 15, 16, 17), sm, k13 (14, 15, 16, 17), sm] 4 times.

➤ continued

- Tapestry needle
- Cotton needlepoint thread to match yarn for seams

GAUGE

14 sts × 18 rows = 4" in St st, unblocked

14 sts × 20 rows = 4" in Staggered Rib Pattern, unblocked

SKILLS USED

Knitting in the round, using multiple stitches to create different textures, cable cast-on

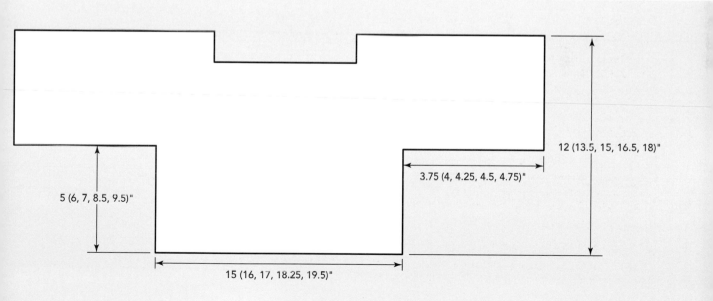

12 (13.5, 15, 16.5, 18)"

3.75 (4, 4.25, 4.5, 4.75)"

5 (6, 7, 8.5, 9.5)"

15 (16, 17, 18.25, 19.5)"

Rep last 2 rows 7 (8, 9, 10, 11) times more.

Next row (RS): [P13 (14, 15, 16, 17), sm, k13 (14, 15, 16, 17), sm] 4 times.

Next row (WS): [K13 (14, 15, 16, 17), sm, p13 (14, 15, 16, 17), sm] 4 times.

Rep last 2 rows 5 (6, 7, 8, 9) times more.

Shape Neck

Next row (RS): Continue in patt for 3 sections, BO 26 (28, 30, 32, 34) sts, removing markers where necessary. Continue in patt to end of row.

Next row (WS): P13 (14, 15, 16, 17), sm, k13 (14, 15, 16, 17), sm, p13 (14, 15, 16, 17), turn.

Continue in patt for 3 more rows.

Next row (WS): BO.

With WS facing, attach yarn to sts for left neck and work 4 rows in patt as set.

Next row (WS): BO.

Top Back and Sleeves

Tranfer 52 (56, 60, 64, 68) held sts to working needle.

With RS facing, attach yarn, pm, and, using cable cast-on method, CO 13 (14, 15, 16, 17) sts, pm, CO another 13 (14, 15, 16, 17) sts.

Continuing on the RS, [K13 (14, 15, 16, 17), sm, p13 (14, 15, 16, 17), sm] 3 times; turn.

Next row (WS): Pm, and, using the cable cast-on method, CO 13 (14, 15, 16, 17) sts, pm, CO another 13 (14, 15, 16, 17) sts. 104 (112, 120, 128, 136) sts.

Continuing on WS, [K13 (14, 15, 16, 17), sm, p13 (14, 15, 16, 17), sm] 4 times.

Next row (RS): [P13 (14, 15, 16, 17), sm, k13 (14, 15, 16, 17), sm] 4 times.

Rep these 2 rows 7 (8, 9, 10, 11) times more.

Next row (RS): [P13 (14, 15, 16, 17), sm, k13 (14, 15, 16, 17), sm] 4 times.

Next row (WS): [K13 (14, 15, 16, 17), sm, p13 (14, 15, 16, 17), sm] 4 times.

Rep these 2 rows 5 (6, 7, 8, 9) times more.

Next row (RS): Work across first 3 sections in patt, BO 26 (28, 30, 32, 34) sts removing markers where necessary, continue in patt to end of row.

Next row (WS): P13 (14, 15, 16, 17), sm, k13 (14, 15, 16, 17), sm, p13 (14, 15, 16, 17), turn.

Continue in patt for 3 more rows.

Next row (WS): BO.

With WS facing, attach yarn to rem sts at neck edge and continue in patt for 4 rows.

Next row (WS): BO.

finishing

With WS facing, sew the shoulder seams and underarm seams. This will create a visible seam to the outside of the shoulders and underarms.

NOTE So that the seams are not too bulky, use a cotton needlepoint thread in the predominant color of the yarn to sew the seams together.

Blocking is not necessary; however, light steaming of the finished garment is optional. Weave in all tails.

CARDIGANS

GINNY
tie-front shrug

GINNY
tie-front shrug

by janine le cras

Ginny is a pretty shrug with trumpet sleeves. It's the perfect garment to keep the little princess in your life from catching a chill. Knit from the top down with a tie front, this shrug knits up in a jiffy and looks equally cute over a T-shirt with jeans or paired with the matching sun top, Hermione.

pattern notes

Please note that this yarn is knitted with a larger needle than recommended on the yarn label in order to create more drape in the fabric. For the backward loop cast-on and picking up stitches, please refer to the "Special Knitting Techniques" appendix.

Garter st in the round: Alternate knit and purl rounds.

directions

This shrug is worked in one piece with raglan shaping, starting at the neck.

CO 41 (41, 41, 46, 49, 51) sts.

Set-up Row (RS): Kfb, yo, place marker (pm), k1, yo, k7 (7, 7, 8, 8, 9), yo, pm, k1, yo, k21 (21, 21, 24, 27, 27), yo, pm, k1, yo, k7 (7, 7, 8, 8, 9), yo, pm, k1, yo, kfb. 10 sts inc'd. 51 (51, 51, 56, 59, 61) sts.

Next row (WS): Purl.

Row 1 (RS): Kfb, k to marker, *yo, slip marker (sm), k1, yo, knit to next marker, rep from * 3 times, k to last st, kfb.

Row 2: Purl.

SIZE
2 (4, 6, 8, 10, 12)

FINISHED MEASUREMENTS
Chest circumference:
21 (23, 25, 26.5, 28, 30)"
Back Length: 5.5 (6.5, 7.5, 9.5, 11, 12)"

MATERIALS
- Madelinetosh *Tosh Sock* (100% superwash merino wool; 395 yd. per 100g skein); color: Tomato; 1 (1, 2, 2, 2, 3) skeins
- US 4 (3.5mm) circular needle, 24" length *(or size needed to match gauge)*
- US 4 (3.5mm) double-pointed needles

continued ➤

- Stitch markers
- Scrap yarn or stitch holders
- Tapestry needle

GAUGE
24 sts × 32 rows = 4" in St st, blocked

SKILLS USED
Basic increasing and decreasing, picking up stitches, knitting in the round, backward loop or cable cast-on

Work Rows 1 and 2 a further 16 (18, 19, 21, 23, 25) times. 211 (231, 241, 266, 289, 311) sts.

separate sleeves and body

Next row (RS): Kfb, k to first marker, *remove marker and place 41 (45, 47, 52, 56, 61) sleeve sts on scrap yarn or holder, remove second marker, CO 8 (8, 8, 10, 10, 12) sts for the underarm using cable or backward loop cast-on*, k across back sts, rep from * to *, k to last st, kfb. 147 (159, 165, 184, 199, 215) sts.

body

Continue body in St st, inc at beg and end of EVERY row (continue with kfb at the beginning and end of RS rows; work first and last sts as pfb on WS rows) until body measures 1 (1.5, 2.25, 3.75, 4.75, 5.25)" from underarm.

Knit 5 rows for garter st edging.

BO.

sleeves

Transfer sts for first sleeve onto dpns. With RS facing, attach yarn and knit across all sts, pick up and knit 8 (8, 8, 10, 10, 12) sts along the underarm. Join sts to work in the round, making sure to pm in middle of picked-up underarm sts to indicate beg of round. 49 (53, 55, 62, 66, 73) sts.

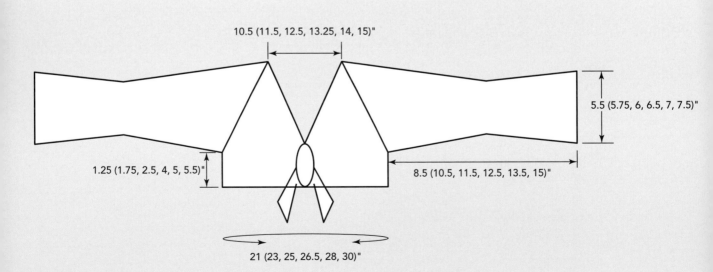

10.5 (11.5, 12.5, 13.25, 14, 15)"

5.5 (5.75, 6, 6.5, 7, 7.5)"

1.25 (1.75, 2.5, 4, 5, 5.5)"

8.5 (10.5, 11.5, 12.5, 13.5, 15)"

21 (23, 25, 26.5, 28, 30)"

Knit 8 rounds.

Next round: Ssk, k to last 2 sts, k2tog.

Rep these 9 rounds 3 (4, 4, 5, 5, 6) more times. 41 (43, 45, 50, 54, 59) sts.

Rearrange the sts evenly on the dpns as follows: 10, 10, 10, 11 ([11, 11, 11, 10], [11, 11, 11, 12], [12, 12, 13, 13], [13, 13, 14, 14], [15, 15, 15, 14]).

Knit 8 rounds.

Next round: On each needle, k1, m1, k to end of needle. 4 sts inc'd.

Rep these 9 rounds 2 (3, 3, 4, 4, 5) more times. 53 (59, 61, 70, 74, 83) sts.

Work 5 rounds in garter st starting with a purl round.

BO all sts.

Rep for second sleeve.

finishing

Weave in all ends. Block to the measurements given in the schematic.

JACK
hooded sweater

JACK
hooded sweater

by lisa s. rowe

The designer's son has worn a zip-front hoodie to school almost every day for the past four years! She also inherited a very similar sweater knit by her grandmother for her dad over forty years ago. Clearly, it's a timeless style much in demand for boys (and girls!) everywhere. This version knits up quickly in a worsted-weight blend and is knit in one piece from the neck down. It gets all the details right: the pockets, hood, and zipper closure make this jacket one that will be worn every day!

pattern notes

For specific instructions on RLI, LLI, and M1P increases; cast-on methods; three-needle bind-off; and mattress stitch, please refer to the "Special Knitting Techniques" appendix.

Instead of wrapping stitches during short-row shaping, this pattern uses yarn overs at the turning points. When you encounter the yarn over in following rows, you will knit or purl it together with the next stitch. This solves two common problems, wrapping too tightly and failing to pick up the wrap with the stitch later.

YOB (backward yarn over)

During the short-row neck shaping, when purl side is facing, move yarn to back before working the next purl st. This will create a yarn over. This backward yarn over creates a stitch that is the same size as a normal yarn over worked on the knit side.

SIZE
4 (6, 8, 10, 12)

FINISHED MEASUREMENTS
Chest circumference: 32 (34, 36, 38, 40)"
Length: 18.75 (20.5, 22, 24, 25.5)"

MATERIALS
- Artful Yarns *Cliché* (55% cotton, 30% linen, 15% acrylic; 112 yd. per 50g ball); color: 19 Sticky Wicket; 8 (8, 9, 9, 10) balls
- US 6 (4mm) circular needle, 24" length *(or size needed to match gauge)*
- US 6 (4mm) double-pointed needles
- US 4 (3.5mm) straight or circular needles

continued ➤

➤ continued

- Smooth scrap yarn
- 4 stitch markers
- 2 stitch holders
- Tapestry needle
- Separating sport zipper, 18 (20, 22, 22, 24)" length
- Sewing thread, needle, and straight pins for zipper

GAUGE
20 sts × 29 rows = 4" in St st, on larger needles, after machine washing

SKILLS USED
Provisional cast-on, increasing and decreasing, short rows, backward yarn over (YOB), backward loop cast-on, picking up stitches, three-needle bind-off, sewing in zipper

directions
upper body

With provisional cast-on and scrap yarn, CO 69 (73, 77, 81, 85) sts to larger needle. Join main yarn and knit 1 row.

Next row (RS): K to last 2 sts, k2tog. 68 (72, 76, 80, 84) sts.

Next row (WS): K3, p to last 3 sts, k3.

Change to smaller needles.

Sizes 4, 8, and 12: K3, (k2, p2) across, end k5.

Sizes 6 and 10: K3, (p2, k2) across, end p2, k3.

Keeping first and last 3 sts in garter st, work in k2, p2 rib for 0.5" ending with a RS row.

Next row (WS): Change to larger needle and k3, p5 (7, 9, 11, 13), place marker (pm), p20, pm, p12, pm, p20, pm, p5 (7, 9, 11, 13), k3.

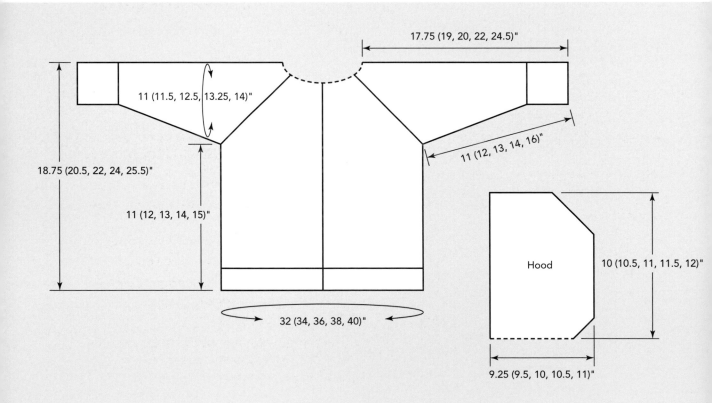

17.75 (19, 20, 22, 24.5)"

11 (11.5, 12.5, 13.25, 14)"

11 (12, 13, 14, 16)"

18.75 (20.5, 22, 24, 25.5)"

11 (12, 13, 14, 15)"

32 (34, 36, 38, 40)"

Hood

10 (10.5, 11, 11.5, 12)"

9.25 (9.5, 10, 10.5, 11)"

You will continue in St st, keeping first and last 3 sts in garter st.

Begin Shaping

You will now begin raglan shaping to create the body and sleeves. At the same time, you will use short rows to shape the neck.

Row 1 (RS): [K to 1 st before next marker, LLI, k1, slip marker (sm), k1, RLI] 3 times, k1, turn.

Row 2 (WS): YOB, p to marker, p14 back neck sts to next marker, p3, turn.

Row 3 (RS): Yo, [k to 1 st before next marker, LLI, k1, sm, k1, RLI] 2 times, k to YOB, slip YOB knitwise, slip next st purlwise, insert LH needle into front of these 2 sts and knit these 2 sts tog, k4 (3, 2, 1, 1), turn.

Row 4 (WS): YOB, p to yo, slip yo knitwise, slip next st knitwise, then purl these 2 sts tog tbl, p4 (3, 2, 1, 1), turn.

Rep last two rows 2 (3, 4, 5, 6) more times. 20 (22, 24, 26, 28) sts between back markers.

Next row (RS): Yo, work to YOB increasing at markers as set, slip YOB knitwise, slip next st purlwise, then knit these 2 sts tog, continue to end of row increasing at marker.

Size 4 only:

Next row (WS): K3, M1P, p to yo, purl yo tog with next st as established, p to last 3 sts, M1P, k3. 2 sts inc'd. 94 sts.

All other sizes:

Next row (WS): K3, p to yo, purl yo tog with next st as established, p to last 3 sts, k3. — (100, 108, 116, 124) sts.

Continue Raglan Shaping

4-st Inc Row (RS): *K to 1 st before marker, LLI, k1, sm, k to next marker, sm, k1, RLI, rep from * once, k to end. 4 sts inc'd.

Next row and following WS rows: K3, p to last 3 sts, k3.

8-st Inc Row (RS): *K to 1 st before marker, LLI, k1, sm, k1, RLI, rep from * 3 times, k to end.

Continue as established, alternating 4-st and 8-st Inc Rows for 30 (34, 38, 42, 46) more rows. 42 (45, 48, 51, 54) sts between sleeve markers.

Rep 4-st Inc Row every RS row 7 (6, 5, 3, 1) more time(s). 33 (35, 38, 40, 42) sts on each front section.

Sizes 4 and 6: Work 2 more rows, inc 1 st at each front only.

Size 8: Work 4 rows even.

Size 10: Work 2 more rows, inc 1 st at each back marker only (78 sts between back markers), then work 4 rows even.

Size 12: Work 4 rows, inc between back markers only (84 sts between back markers), then work 6 rows even.

220 (234, 248, 262, 276) sts.

sleeves

You will work the sleeves flat, one at a time, before you finish the body.

K to first marker, place left front sts on spare needle, k to second marker, CO 7 (8, 8, 9, 9) sts, using backward loop or knitted cast-on, turn, p sleeve sts, CO 7 (7, 8, 8, 9) sts. Transfer remaining sts for body and right sleeve to spare needle or scrap yarn.

Work back and forth in St st on the 56 (60, 64, 68, 72) sleeve sts for 6 (6, 6, 6, 10) rows.

Dec Row (RS): K1, k2tog, k to last 3 sts, ssk, k1.

Rep Dec Row every 8 (10, 10, 12, 12) rows 6 more times. 42 (46, 50, 54, 58) sts.

Work even until sleeve measures 9 (10, 10.5, 11.5, 13)" from underarm. Dec 6 sts evenly spaced across last WS row.

Change to smaller needles and work in k2, p2 rib for 2 (2, 2.5, 2.5, 3)".

BO in rib.

With RS facing, rejoin yarn to back sts, work to next marker, return back sts to spare needle, work second sleeve the same as first, rejoin yarn to right front sts, and k to end of row.

Sew sleeve seams from cuff to underarm.

body

Next row (WS): K3, p right front sts, pick up and purl 12 (13, 14, 15, 16) sts in CO underarm sts, work back sts, pick up and purl 12 (13, 14, 15, 16) sts in CO underarm sts, work left front sts, ending k3.

Keeping edges in garter st as established, work even on 160 (170, 180, 190, 200) sts until piece measures 9 (10, 10.5, 11.5, 12)" from underarm or 2 (2, 2.5, 2.5, 3)" less than desired length, ending with a RS row.

Next row (WS): K3, p1 (4, 3, 6, 1), p2tog, [p8 (7, 9, 8, 8), p2tog] across, end k3. 144 (152, 164, 172, 180) sts.

Change to smaller needle.

Sizes 4, 8, and 12: K3, [k2, p2] across, end k5.

Sizes 6 and 10: K3, [p2, k2] across, end p2, k3.

Continue in rib as set for 2 (2, 2.5, 2.5, 3)".

BO in rib.

hood

Remove provisional cast-on at neck and transfer these 68 (72, 76, 80, 84) sts to larger needle.

Next row (RS): Join yarn; k3, m1, [k5 (5, 5, 6, 6), m1] 6 times, k2 (6, 10, 2, 6), [m1, k5 (5, 5, 6, 6)] 6 times, m1, k3. 14 sts inc'd. 82 (86, 90, 94, 98) sts.

Next row (WS): K3, p to last 3 sts, k3.

Work 2 rows even.

Inc Row (RS): K34 (36, 38, 40, 42) LLI, pm, k14, pm, RLI, k to end.

Inc at markers as set every 4th row 4 more times. Work even on 92 (96, 100, 104, 108) sts until hood measures 8 (8.5, 9, 9.5, 10)" from top of neck ribbing.

Dec Row (RS): K to marker, k2tog, k to next marker, sm, ssk, work to end.

Rep Dec Row every other row 5 more times. 80 (84, 88, 92, 96) sts.

End with a WS row. Place half of sts on each needle and fold hood in half with WS facing. Use three-needle bind-off to close top of hood.

pockets

Right Pocket

With larger needle, CO 26 (28, 30, 32, 34) sts.

Work 14 rows in St st beg with a knit row.

Dec Row (RS): K3, k2tog, k to end.

WS rows: P to last 3 sts, k3.

Rep last 2 rows once, then work 2 rows even.

Rep these 6 rows until piece measures 6 (6.5, 7, 7.5, 8)", then BO.

Left Pocket

CO and work first 14 rows the same as right pocket.

Dec Row (RS): K to last 5 sts, ssk, k3.

WS rows: K3, p to end.

Rep last 2 rows once, then work 2 rows even.

Rep last 6 rows until piece measures 6 (6.5, 7, 7.5, 8)", then BO.

finishing

Sew sleeve seams.

Place pockets on front of garment so that the bottom edge aligns with top of ribbing and the long side of the pocket is just inside the garter st edging. Pin in place, making sure that tops of pockets are even with one another. Sew in place with mattress stitch, and weave in the ends securely at either side of pocket opening.

Weave in loose ends and block lightly. Machine wash and dry if planning to care for garment this way before adding zipper. Machine wash and dry zipper, too, before sewing in place.

install zipper

Working on a flat surface, use straight pins to pin the closed zipper to one inside front edge with bottom edges even, folding tape under and inside at neck edge. Make sure garment edge matches center of zipped zipper. Lay other garment edge next to first, matching top and bottom edges and making sure edges meet in center over zipper teeth. Pin. With needle and thread in contrasting color, baste zipper into place. Remove pins. Check to see if zipper operates properly, and if the garment and zipper tape are lying flat and even. Machine or hand stitch from bottom edge to neck edge in center of garter edging with matching thread. Reinforce/tack well at tops and bottoms. Cut away extra zipper tape at top. Remove basting thread.

ARTEMIS
zip-up jacket

ARTEMIS
zip-up jacket

by anne lecrivain

This easygoing unisex jacket with a bold stripe and nice deep pockets is fun to wear and fun to knit. Choose delicate shades, bright crayon-box colors, or even the colors of your child's favorite team to make a sweater that your child will want to wear again and again.

directions

The jacket is worked from the top down. For knitted and backward loop cast-on techniques as well as picking up stitches, please refer to the "Special Knitting Techniques" appendix.

yoke

With MC, CO 52 (58, 64, 70, 74, 82).

Knit 6 rows in garter st.

Next row (RS): *K1, kfb, rep from * to end of row. 78 (87, 96, 105, 111, 123) sts.

Work 7 (9, 9, 11, 11, 11) rows in St st.

Next row (RS): *K2, kfb, rep from * to end of row. 104 (116, 128, 140, 148, 164) sts.

Next row (WS): Purl.

Switch to CC, knit 2 rows. Work 4 (6, 6, 8, 8, 8) rows in St st.

Next row (RS): Still working in CC, *k3, kfb, rep from * to end of row. 130 (145, 160, 175, 185, 205) sts.

Continue working in CC until you have worked a total of 15 rows (all sizes).

Next row (WS): Switch to MC and knit.

Work 0 (2, 2, 4, 4, 4) rows in St st.

SIZE
2 (4, 6, 8, 10, 12)

FINISHED MEASUREMENTS
Chest circumference:
28 (30, 32, 34, 36, 38)"
Length: 14.5 (17, 19, 20.5, 21.5, 22.5)"

MATERIALS
- Berroco *Weekend* (75% acrylic, 25% Peruvian cotton; 205 yd. per 100g skein); [MC] color: 5923 Tomatillo, 3 (3, 4, 4, 4, 5) skeins; [CC] color: 5930 Steel Blue, 1 skein (all sizes)
- US 8 (5mm) circular needle, 24" length (*or size needed to match gauge*)
- US 8 (5mm) double-pointed needles

continued ➤

➤ continued

- Separating zipper
- Sewing thread to match CC

GAUGE

18 sts × 24 rows = 4" in St st, unblocked

SKILLS USED

Increasing and decreasing, picking up stitches, backward loop or knitted cast-on

Next row (RS): *K4, kfb, rep from * to end of row. 156 (174, 192, 210, 222, 246) sts.

Work even in St st on yoke until piece measures 6.5 (7.5, 7.5, 8, 8, 8)" from CO edge.

Divide Body and Sleeves

Next row (RS): K25 (27, 30, 31, 34, 36), place next 27 (33, 36, 42, 42, 51) sts on a holder or scrap yarn, CO 12 sts using knitted or backward loop cast on, k52 (54, 60, 64, 70, 72), place next 27 (33, 36, 42, 42, 51) sts on a holder or scrap yarn, CO 12, k to end. 126 (132, 144, 150, 162, 168) sts.

Continue in St st until piece measures 10.5 (12.5, 13.5, 14.5, 15, 15.5)".

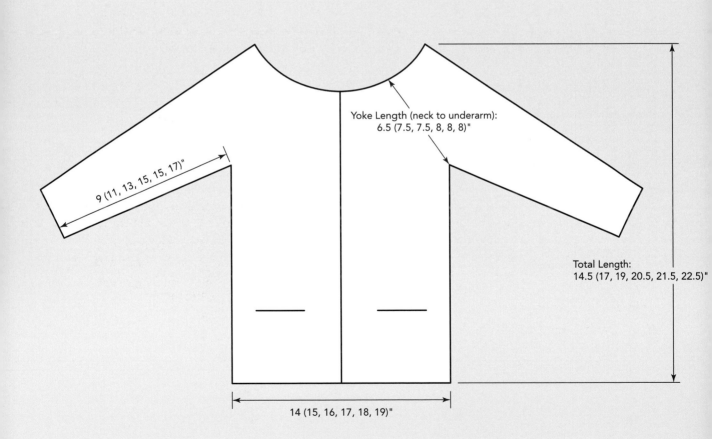

9 (11, 13, 15, 15, 17)"

Yoke Length (neck to underarm):
6.5 (7.5, 7.5, 8, 8, 8)"

Total Length:
14.5 (17, 19, 20.5, 21.5, 22.5)"

14 (15, 16, 17, 18, 19)"

Make Pocket Openings

Next Row (RS): K6 (7, 7, 8, 8, 9), BO 13 (13, 16, 16, 17, 18), k to last 19 (20, 23, 24, 25, 27) sts, BO 13 (13, 16, 16, 17, 18), k to end.

Next Row (WS): P6 (7, 7, 8, 8, 9), CO 13 (13, 16, 16, 17, 18), p to bound-off sts, CO 13 (13, 16, 16, 17, 18), p 6 (7, 7, 8, 8, 9).

Continue to work in St st until piece measures 14 (16.5, 18.5, 20, 21, 22)" or 0.5" shorter than desired length.

Knit 6 rows.

BO.

sleeves

Transfer 27 (33, 36, 42, 42, 51) sts held for first sleeve to dpns. Pick up and knit 6 sts from cast-on underarm sts, pm to mark beg of round, pick up and knit 6 more sts under the arm. Join to work in the round and continue in St st, working following Dec Round every 5th (7th, 7th, 14th, 14th, 11th) round 6 (9, 10, 6, 6, 8) times: K1, ssk, knit to last 3 sts, k2tog, k1.

Work even in St st until sleeve measures 8.5 (10.5, 12.5, 14.5, 14.5, 16.5)" or 0.5" shorter than desired length.

Work 6 rounds of garter st (knit 1 round, purl 1 round).

BO.

Rep for second sleeve.

pockets

Make both pockets the same way.

With RS facing, using dpns and CC, pick up and knit 13 (13, 16, 16, 17, 18) sts across top of pocket opening (the top as the sweater will be worn).

Work in St st for 3.5 (4, 5, 5.5, 6, 6.5)". BO.

Across the bottom of the same pocket opening, with CC pick up and knit 13 (13, 16, 16, 17, 18) sts.

Knit 6 rows for garter st edging. BO.

Sew remaining three sides of the pocket flap to inside of sweater front. Sew the short edges of pocket edging to the RS of the sweater. Weave in ends.

front edging

Along right front edge, with CC and RS facing, pick up and knit 2 sts for every 3 rows from hem to neck edge. Knit 6 rows for garter st edging. BO.

Along left front edge, with CC and RS facing, pick up and knit the same number of sts from neck edge to hem. Knit 6 rows. BO.

finishing

Weave in ends and block if desired.

insert zipper

Choose a zipper the same length as the finished front opening (take the sweater with you to purchase the zipper). If necessary, the top of the zipper can be trimmed and stitched down.

Pin each side of the separating zipper to the respective side, and, using sewing thread and needle, attach zipper with small stitches sewn down the center of the zipper tape.

SATSUKI
yukata robe

SATSUKI
yukata robe
by sarah barbour

Ⓘn Japan, the *yukata,* along with fireworks, handheld fans, and fizzy lemonade, is a symbol of summer. Both children and adults are seen wearing these casual, comfortable robes at any summer festival, and the sight of them remains one of designer Sarah Barbour's favorite memories of her years spent in Japan. Your girl will be delighted to wear Satsuki as a cover-up after a swim or as a lightweight coat that's perfect for special occasions.

pattern notes

This robe is worked back and forth in pieces and then seamed. You will pick up stitches around the neckline and then knit the collar.

Intarsia: Work each color section with a separate length (or bobbin) of yarn. Some sections, like flower centers, will only use short lengths of approximately 1–2 yds. Be sure to twist the two strands of yarn around each other when switching between colors to avoid gaps.

All charts in this pattern are available for download at www.wiley.com/go/moreknittinginthesun.

SIZE
2–4 (6–8, 10–12)

FINISHED MEASUREMENTS
Chest circumference: 25.5 (34, 43)"
Length: 16 (19.25, 21.25)"

MATERIALS
- Rowan *Wool Cotton* (50% merino wool, 50% cotton; 123 yd. per 50g ball); [MC] color: 901 Citron, 8 (10, 11) balls; [A] color: 952 Hiss 1 (2, 2) ball(s); [B] color: 900 Antique, 1 ball; [C] color: 974 Freesia, 1 ball
- US 5 (3.75mm) straight or circular needles (*or size needed to match gauge*)
- US 4 (3.5mm) circular needle, 24" length or longer

continued ➤

➤ **continued**

- Bobbins, optional
- Tapestry needle

GAUGE
21 sts × 29 rows = 4" in St st on
larger needles, unblocked

SKILLS USED
Intarsia, basic increasing and
decreasing, picking up stitches

directions
back

With MC and smaller needles, CO 68 (90, 114) sts.

Beg with a knit row, work 5 rows in St st.

Knit 1 WS row for turning ridge.

Switch to larger needles and beg Back Intarsia Chart at row designated for your size. Work through row 123 (141, 163).

BO.

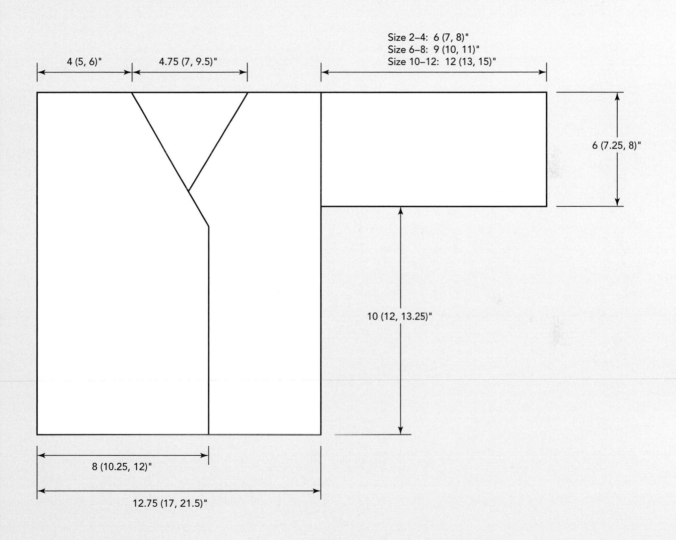

Size 2–4: 6 (7, 8)"
Size 6–8: 9 (10, 11)"
Size 10–12: 12 (13, 15)"

4 (5, 6)"

4.75 (7, 9.5)"

6 (7.25, 8)"

10 (12, 13.25)"

8 (10.25, 12)"

12.75 (17, 21.5)"

Back Intarsia Chart

Right Front Intarsia Chart

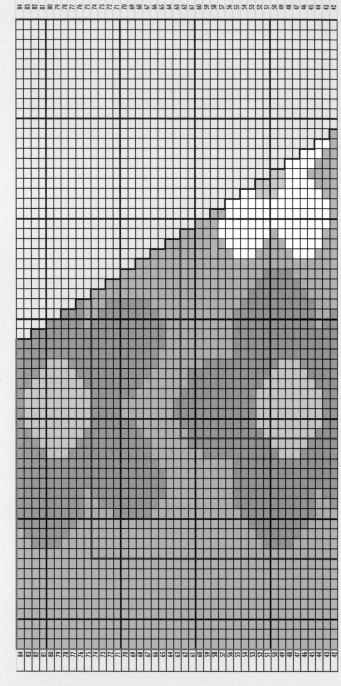

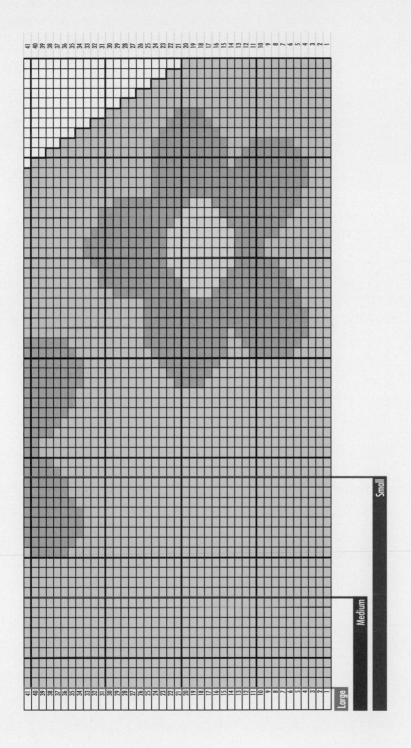

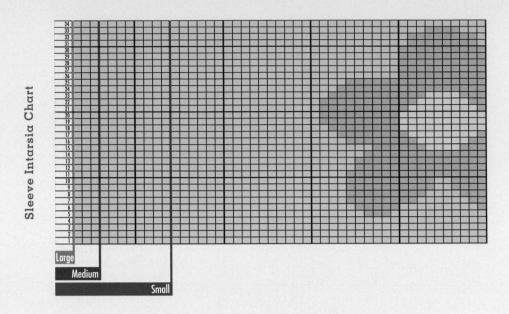

Sleeve Intarsia Chart

Large
Medium
Small

left front

The left front is worked entirely with MC.

With smaller needles, CO 42 (54, 64).

Beg with a knit row, work 5 rows in St st.

Knit 1 WS row for turning ridge.

Switch to larger needles and work 74 (88, 100) rows in St st.

Shape Neckline

Next row (RS): K to last 4 sts, ssk, k2. Place a removable marker or length of scrap yarn on this row for later collar shaping.

Next row (WS): Purl.

Rep these 2 rows until there are 21 (26, 32) sts on needle.

BO.

right front

With MC and smaller needles, CO 42 (54, 64).

Beg with a knit row, work 5 rows in St st.

Knit 1 WS row for turning ridge.

Switch to larger needles and work 54 (68, 80) rows even in St st with MC, then begin Right Front Intarsia Chart as indicated for your size.

Beg at Row 21 of chart, work neckline shaping on RS rows as foll: K2, k2tog, k to end. Place a removable marker to mark the first row of shaping.

Continue following chart and dec as set every RS row until 21 (26, 32) sts rem.

BO.

sleeves

(make 2)

With MC and smaller needles, CO 63 (78, 85).

Beg with a knit row, work 5 rows in St st.

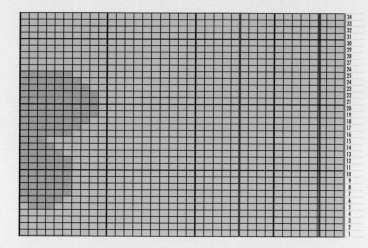

Knit 1 WS row for turning ridge.

Switch to larger needles and beg Sleeve Intarsia Chart according to your size. When the 34 rows of the chart are complete, continue in MC and St st until sleeve measures 6 (9, 12)" for the younger or smaller end of the size range. For older and taller children, work even for 1–3" more. Sleeve measures 6 [7, 8] (9 [10, 11], 12 [13, 15]".

ties

(make 2)

With Color B and smaller needles, CO 10 sts. Work in k1, p1 rib until tie measures 5 (7, 8)". BO.

finishing

Weave in ends. Block all pieces. Sew fronts to back at shoulders. Sew arms to body. Sew right side seam. Sew left side seam, sewing in one tie just below the sleeve. Turn hems to WS at turning ridge and sew in place on WS.

collar

With RS facing, starting at bottom right front, using smaller circular needle, pick up and knit 5 sts per inch up right front, across back collar and down left front. Move markers indicating beg of neckline shaping to nearest picked up sts.

Row 1 (WS): Purl.

Row 2 (RS): *K to marked st, m1, k1, m1; rep from * once, k to end.

Row 3: Purl.

Row 4: Knit.

Rep these 4 rows 1 (2, 2) time(s) more.

Knit 1 WS row for turning ridge.

Begin Collar Facing

Row 1: *K to 2 sts before marked st, ssk, k1, k2tog; rep from * once, k to end.

Row 2: Purl.

Row 3: Knit.

Row 4: Purl.

Rep these 4 rows 1 (2, 2) time(s) more.

BO loosely.

Sew down BO edge to inside collar. Weave in all ends.

Sew second tie in place just below the beginning of neckline shaping.

BEEZUS
cropped lace jacket

by katherine vaughan

This cropped cardigan has an open front with I-cord ties and a simple overall diamond lace pattern. It's great over a camisole or tee, or pair it with its companion tank, Ramona, for a put-together look ready for any occasion.

pattern notes

This pattern uses a single crochet edging around the cuffs and hem. If you prefer, you can substitute attached I-cord for a similar look. For crochet and I-cord techniques, see the "Special Knitting Techniques" appendix.

All charts in this pattern are available for download at **www.wiley.com/go/moreknittinginthesun**.

beezus body stitch

(worked over a multiple of 8 sts)

Row 1 and all WS rows (WS): Purl.

Row 2: Knit.

Row 4: *K5, yo, ssk, k1; rep from * to end.

Row 6: *K4, yo, s2kp, yo, k1; rep from * to end.

Row 8: *K4, k2tog, yo, k2; rep from * to end.

Row 10: Knit.

Row 12: *K1, yo, ssk, k5; rep from * to end.

Row 14: *Yo, s2kp, yo, k5; rep from * to end.

Row 16: *K2tog, yo, k6; rep from * to end.

Rep these 16 rows for patt.

SIZE
2 (4, 6, 8, 10, 12)

FINISHED MEASUREMENTS
Chest circumference:
22.5 (24.5, 27, 28.5, 30, 32.5)"
Length: 7 (8, 9, 10.5, 11.5, 12.5)"

MATERIALS
- Classic Elite *Allegoro* (70% organic cotton, 30% linen; 152 yd. per 50g ball); color: 5634 Best Berry; 3 (3, 4, 4, 5, 5) balls
- US 3 (3.25mm) straight needles
- US 3 (3.25mm) double-pointed needles
- Size D (3.25mm) crochet hook
- Stitch holder or scrap yarn
- Tapestry needle

continued ➤

beezus sleeve stitch

(worked over a multiple of 8 sts + 4)

Row 1 and all WS rows (WS): Purl.

Row 2: Knit.

Row 4: *K5, yo, ssk, k1; rep from * to last 4 sts, k4.

Row 6: *K4, yo, s2kp, yo, k1; rep from * to last 4 sts, k4.

Row 8: *K4, k2tog, yo, k2; rep from * to last 4 sts, k4.

Row 10: Knit.

Row 12: *K1, yo, ssk, k5; rep from * to last 4 sts, k1, yo, ssk, k1.

Row 14: *Yo, s2kp, yo, k5; rep from * to last 4 sts, yo, s2kp, yo, k1.

Row 16: *K2tog, yo, k6; rep from * to last 4 sts, k2tog, yo, k2.

Rep these 16 rows for patt.

directions

back

With straight needles, CO 64 (70, 78, 82, 86, 94) sts.

Row 1 (WS): P0 (3, 3, 1, 3, 3), beg working Beezus Body Stitch with Row 1 across, end P0 (3, 3, 1, 3, 3).

Work even in Beezus Body Stitch with 0 (3, 3, 1, 3, 3) selvedge sts on *each* side worked in St st until back measures 1 (1.5, 1.5, 2.5, 3, 3.5)" from CO edge, ending with a WS row.

Shape Armholes

Continue working in Beezus Body Stitch patt throughout.

BO 2 (3, 3, 4, 4, 5) at beg of next 2 rows. 60 (64, 72, 74, 78, 84) sts.

BO 2 (2, 3, 3, 3, 3) at beg of next 2 rows.

BO 1 (1, 2, 2, 2, 2) at beg of next 2 rows.

BO 0 (1, 2, 1, 1, 2) at beg of next 2 rows.

BO 0 (0, 1, 1, 1, 1) at beg of next 2 rows. 54 (56, 58, 60, 64, 68) sts.

Work even in patt until back measures 6 (7, 8, 9.5, 10.5, 11.5)" from CO edge, ending with a WS row.

➤ **continued**

GAUGE

25 sts × 39 rows = 4" in St st, blocked

23 sts × 41 rows = 4" in Beezus Body Stitch, blocked

SKILLS USED

Basic lace, basic shaping, I-cord and attached I-cord, single crochet edging, seaming

Beezus Body Stitch Chart

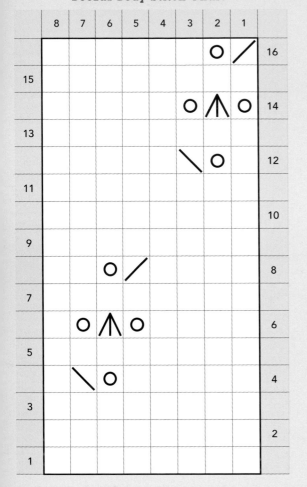

Beezus Sleeve Stitch Chart

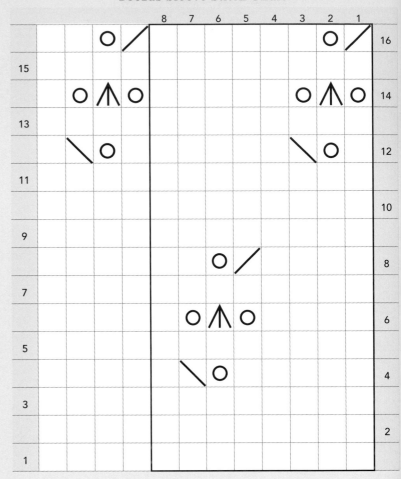

Key to Beezus Stitch Charts

knit
RS: knit
WS: purl

yo
yarn over

ssk
Slip 1 stitch as if to knit, slip another stitch as if to knit. Insert LH needle into front of these 2 stitches and knit them together.

s2kp
Slip 2 sts as if to k2tog, k1, pass slipped sts over st just knit.

k2tog
Knit 2 stitches together as 1 stitch.

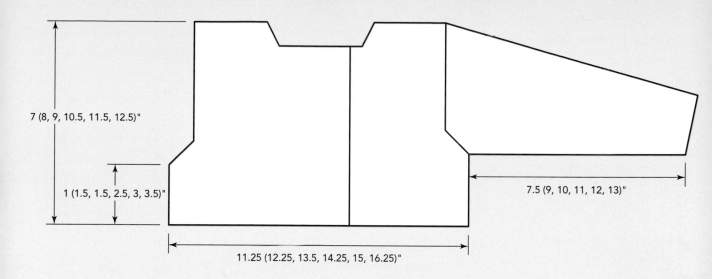

7 (8, 9, 10.5, 11.5, 12.5)"

1 (1.5, 1.5, 2.5, 3, 3.5)"

7.5 (9, 10, 11, 12, 13)"

11.25 (12.25, 13.5, 14.25, 15, 16.25)"

Shape Neckline

Next row (RS): Work 16 (17, 18, 19, 20, 21) sts in patt and place them on holder or scrap yarn for right shoulder, BO 22 (22, 22, 22, 24, 26) sts, work in patt to end.

Left Neck

Row 1 and all WS rows: Purl.

Row 2: BO 3, work in patt to end.

Row 4: BO 2, work in patt to end.

Row 6: BO 1, work in patt to end.

Row 8: BO rem 10 (11, 12, 13, 14, 15) sts.

Right Neck

Transfer sts held for right shoulder to working needles and join new yarn at the armhole edge. Shaping will be done on WS (purl) rows.

Row 1 and all RS rows: Work in patt.

Row 2: BO 3, p to end.

Row 4: BO 2, p to end.

Row 6: BO 1, p to end.

Row 8: BO rem 10 (11, 12, 13, 14, 15) sts.

left front

With straight needles, CO 25 (28, 33, 34, 35, 38) sts.

Row 1 (WS): P1 (2, 1, 1, 2, 3), beg working Beezus Body Stitch with Row 1, end p0 (2, 0, 1, 1, 3).

Work even in Beezus Body Stitch, maintaining selvedge sts on each side as set until left front measures 1 (1.5, 1.5, 2.5, 3, 3.5)" from CO edge, ending with a WS row.

Shape Armhole

Continue working in Beezus Sleeve Stitch patt throughout.

Row 1 (RS): BO 2 (3, 3, 4, 4, 5), work in patt to end. 23 (25, 30, 30, 31, 33) sts rem.

Row 2 and all WS rows: Purl.

Row 3: BO 2 (2, 3, 3, 3, 3), work in patt to end.

Row 5: BO 1 (1, 2, 2, 2, 2), work in patt to end.

Row 7: BO 0 (1, 2, 1, 1, 2), work in patt to end.

Row 9: BO 0 (0, 1, 1, 1, 1), work in patt to end. 20 (21, 22, 23, 24, 25) sts.

Work even in patt until front measures 4.5 (5.5, 6, 7, 7.5, 8)" from CO edge, ending with a WS row.

Shape Neckline

Row 1 and all RS rows: Work in patt.

Row 2 (WS): BO 4 (4, 4, 4, 4, 4), p to end. 16 (17, 18, 19, 20, 21) sts.

Row 4: BO 3, p to end.

Row 6: BO 2, p to end.

Row 8: BO 1, p to end. 10 (11, 12, 13, 14, 15) sts rem.

Work even in patt until front measures 7 (8, 9, 10.5, 11.5, 12.5)" or same as back.

BO.

right front

With straight needles, CO 25 (28, 33, 34, 35, 38) sts.

Row 1 (WS): P0 (2, 0, 1, 1, 3). Beg working Beezus Stitch (body) with Row 1, end p1 (2, 1, 1, 2, 3).

Work even in Beezus st, maintaining selvedge sts on each side as set until right front measures 1 (1.5, 1.5, 2.5, 3, 3.5)" from CO edge, ending with a RS row.

Shape Armhole

Continue working in Beezus Sleeve Stitch patt throughout.

Row 1 (WS): BO 2 (3, 3, 4, 4, 5), p to end. 23 (25, 30, 30, 31, 33) sts.

Row 2 and all RS rows: Work in patt to end.

Row 3: BO 2 (2, 3, 3, 3, 3) p to end.

Row 5: BO 1 (1, 2, 2, 2, 2), p to end.

Row 7: BO 0 (1, 2, 1, 1, 2), p to end.

Row 9: BO 0 (0, 1, 1, 1, 1), p to end. 20 (21, 22, 23, 24, 25) sts.

Work even in patt until front measures 4.5 (5.5, 6, 7, 7.5, 8)" from CO edge, ending with a RS row.

Shape Neckline

Row 1 and all WS rows: Purl.

Row 2: BO 4 (4, 4, 4, 5, 6), p to end.

Row 4: BO 3, work to end.

Row 6: BO 2, work to end.

Row 8: BO 1, work to end. 10 (11, 12, 13, 14, 15) sts.

Work even in patt until right front measures 7 (8, 9, 10.5, 11.5, 12.5)" or same as left front.

BO.

sleeves

(make 2)

As you increase, incorporate new sts into Beezus Sleeve Stitch patt.

With straight needles, CO 40 (42, 48, 56, 56, 64) sts.

Row 1 (WS): P2 (3, 2, 2, 2, 2), beg working Beezus Sleeve Stitch with Row 1, end p2 (3, 2, 2, 2, 2). Continue working Rows 2–9 of patt maintaining selvedge sts.

Next Row (Row 10): K1, m1, work in patt to last st, m1, k1.

Work 7 rows in patt.

Next Row (Row 2): K1, m1, work in patt to last st, m1, k1.

Work 7 rows in patt.

Continue in patt, inc every 8 rows (Rows 2 and 10 of Beezus Sleeve Stitch patt) until there are 54 (60, 72, 78, 80, 90) sts, ending with Row 1 or Row 9.

Shape Sleeve Cap

Continue in Beezus Sleeve Stitch pattern as you shape the sleeve cap.

BO 2 (3, 3, 4, 4, 5) at beg of next 2 rows.
50 (54, 66, 70, 72, 80) sts.

BO 2 (2, 3, 3, 3, 3) at beg of next 2 rows.

BO 1 (1, 2, 2, 2, 2) at beg of next 2 rows.

BO 0 (1, 2, 1, 1, 2) at beg of next 2 rows.

BO 0 (0, 1, 1, 1, 1) at beg of next 2 rows.
44 (46, 50, 56, 58, 64) sts.

Work 4 rows even.

BO 1 st at beg of next 22 rows.
22 (24, 28, 34, 36, 42) sts.

BO 1 (1, 1, 2, 2, 2) at beg of next 2 rows.

BO 2 (2, 3, 3, 3, 4) at beg of next 2 rows.

BO 3 (3, 3, 4, 4, 5) at beg of next 2 rows.

BO rem 10 (12, 14, 16, 18, 20) sts.

finishing

Weave in ends and block to measurements given in schematic.

Sew shoulder and side seams. Sew sleeve seams. Ease sleeves into armholes and sew into place.

Using crochet hook, work sc edging starting at left front neckline corner down the left front, around the hem, and up the right front, ending at the right front corner. *Note:* Work 3 sc into the corners between the hem and the fronts for a crisper corner.

Work sc edging around the cuffs.

i-cord ties

With dpns, CO 3 sts.

Work I-Cord for 11", slightly stretched.

Continue as attached I-cord trim, starting at left front neckline corner, continuing around the back of the neck, and finishing at right front neckline corner.

Work I-cord for 11" more, slightly stretched.

BO all sts.

Weave in ends and trim.

Block.

NATKA
openwork cardigan

by faina goberstein

This cropped openwork cardigan is so breezy and easy to wear, your child will throw it on with everything! This sweater is worked in one piece from the bottom up. The back and both fronts above the armhole are worked in two mirror-image lace patterns that meet at center back and center front. Garter stitch is used as trim at the neckline, sleeve edges, shoulders, and hem. A short buttonhole band finishes the look.

pattern notes

This cardigan is knit as one piece from the bottom up to the armhole. Stitches for sleeves are cast on and worked with the back stitches. Make sure to follow the pattern and charts carefully. Measure buttonhole band as you work on it so it matches up exactly with the length of the front.

All charts in this pattern are available for download at **www.wiley.com/go/moreknittinginthesun**.

decreases

Sl 1 – ssk – psso (left-leaning double decrease): Sl 1 st knitwise, ssk (sl 2 sts knitwise, 1 at a time, then insert LH needle into fronts of these 2 sts and knit them together), pass the first slipped st over the st just made.

When decreasing for neck over Right-Slanting Madeira Lace: When you do not have sufficient sts to work "yo, k3tog, yo," after your initial decrease at the beginning of the row, then begin the row with "sl 1, ssk, k2tog, yo" instead. The next decrease row will omit both yarn overs. Work it as "sl 1, ssk. . . ."

SIZE
2 (4, 6, 8, 10)

FINISHED MEASUREMENTS
Chest circumference: 22 (25, 28, 31, 35)"
Length: 7 (8, 10, 11, 12)"

MATERIALS
- Berroco *Vintage Wool* (50% acrylic, 40% wool, 10% nylon; 217 yd. per 100g skein); color: 5113 Misty; 2 (2, 3, 3, 4) skeins
- US 6 (4mm) circular needle, 24" length (*or size needed to match gauge*)
- Stitch markers
- Stitch holders or scrap yarn

continued ➤

➤ **continued**

- Tapestry needle
- Sewing needle and thread
- Sizes 2 and 4: two buttons, 0.5"
- Sizes 6, 8, and 10: three buttons, 0.75"

GAUGE

22 sts × 32 rows = 4" in Rickrack Lace, blocked

21 sts × 32 rows = 4" in Madeira Lace, blocked

20 sts × 34 rows = 4" in garter st, blocked

SKILLS USED

Lace knitting, chart reading, decreasing in lace pattern, three-needle bind-off, twisted backward loop cast-on

When decreasing for neck over Left-Slanting Madeira Lace: If you cannot work the *final* yarn over of "yo, sl 1 – ssk – psso, yo" before the decrease, then work the end of the row as " . . . yo, ssk, k2tog." You will omit both yarn overs on the next decrease row. Work it as " . . . k2tog."

twisted backward loop cast-on

This CO is done at the end of a row. Hold RH needle with your right hand. With your left hand make a loop out of working yarn; twist it one more time. Put the loop on the needle backwards. The extra twist tightens the CO row.

rickrack lace

(worked over a multiple of 8 sts)

Row 1 (RS): *P2, k2tog, yo, p2, k2; rep from * to end.

Rows 2 and 4: *P2, k2; rep from * to end.

Row 3: *P2, yo, ssk, p2, k2; rep from * to end.

Rep these 4 rows for patt.

right-slanting madeira lace

(worked over a multiple of 4 sts + 5)

Row 1 and all WS rows: Purl.

Row 2: K2, yo, *k3tog, yo, k1, yo; rep from * to last 3 sts, k3tog, yo.

Row 4: K1, yo, k3tog, *yo, k1, yo, k3tog; rep from * to last st, yo, k1.

Row 6: K1, k2tog, yo, *k1, yo, k3tog, yo; rep from * to last 2 sts, k2.

Row 8: K2tog, yo, k1, *yo, k3tog, yo, k1; rep from * to last 2 sts, yo, k2tog.

Rep these 8 rows for patt.

Rickrack Lace Chart

	8	7	6	5	4	3	2	1	
4			●	●			●	●	
			●	●	/	O	●	●	3
2			●	●			●	●	
			●	●	O	/	●	●	1

Right-Slanting Madeira Lace Chart

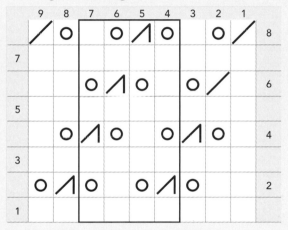

Left-Slanting Madeira Lace Chart

Key to Lace Charts

knit
RS: knit stitch
WS: purl stitch

purl
RS: purl stitch
WS: knit stitch

yo
yarn over

k3tog
Knit 3 stitches together as one.

sl1-ssk-psso
Sl1 st knitwise, ssk, pass the slipped st over the st just made.

k2tog
Knit 2 stitches together.

ssk
Slip 1 stitch as if to knit, slip another stitch as if to knit. Insert LH needle into front of these 2 stitches and knit them together.

left-slanting madeira lace

(worked over a multiple of 4 sts + 5)

Row 1 and all WS rows: Purl.

Row 2: Yo, sl 1 – ssk – psso, *yo,k1, yo, sl 1 – ssk – psso; rep from * to last 2 sts, yo, k2.

Row 4: K1, yo, *sl 1 – ssk – psso, yo, k1, yo; rep from * to last 4 sts, sl 1 – ssk – psso, yo, k1.

Row 6: K2, *yo, sl 1 – ssk – psso, yo, k1; rep from * to last 3 sts, yo, ssk, k1.

Row 8: Ssk, yo, *k1, yo, sl 1 kwise – ssk – psso, yo; rep from * to last 3 sts, k1, yo, ssk.

Rep these 8 rows for patt.

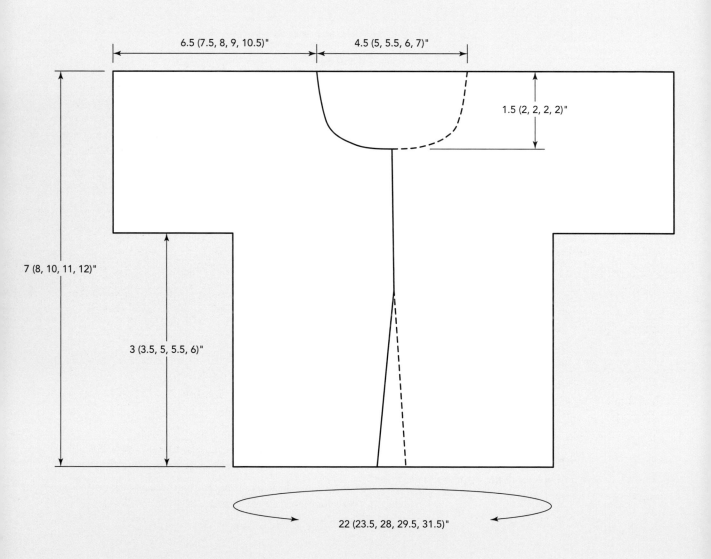

6.5 (7.5, 8, 9, 10.5)"

4.5 (5, 5.5, 6, 7)"

1.5 (2, 2, 2, 2)"

7 (8, 10, 11, 12)"

3 (3.5, 5, 5.5, 6)"

22 (23.5, 28, 29.5, 31.5)"

directions

For M1L and M1R increases, please refer to the "Special Knitting Techniques" appendix.

CO 121 (137, 155, 171, 189) sts.

Row 1: Sl 1 wyif, k to end.

Rep this row 2 more times.

Begin Rickrack Lace as follows:

Next row (RS): Sl 1 wyif, k2 (2, 3, 3, 4), k1, place marker (pm), work Row 1 of Rickrack Lace 7 (8, 9, 10, 11) times, pm, p1, pm, work Row 3 of Rickrack Lace 7 (8, 9, 10, 11) times, pm, k1, turn. Place remaining 3 (3, 4, 4, 5) sts on holder or scrap yarn.

Next row: Sl 1 wyif, work Row 4 of Rickrack Lace 7 (8, 9, 10, 11) times, k1, work Row 2 of Rickrack Lace 7 (8, 9, 10, 11) times, k1. Place rem 3 (3, 4, 4, 5) sts on holder or scrap yarn. 115 (131, 147, 163, 179) sts.

Next row: Sl 1 wyif, work Row 3 of Rickrack Lace to marker, p1, work Row 1 of Rickrack Lace to marker, k1.

Next row: Sl 1 wyif, work Row 2 of Rickrack Lace to marker, k1, Work Row 4 of Rickrack Lace to marker, k1.

Continue working the 4 rows of Rickrack Lace as set between markers 1 (1, 2, 2, 3) more time(s). End with a WS row.

Inc Row (RS): Sl 1 wyif, M1L, slip marker (sm), work Row 1 of Rickrack Lace to marker, p1, Work Row 3 of Rickrack Lace to marker, sm, M1R, k1. 117 (133, 149, 165, 181) sts.

Next row (WS): Sl 1 wyif, p1, work lace patt as set to marker, k1, work lace patt to marker, p1, k1.

Next row: Sl1 wyif, k1, work lace patt as set to marker, p1, work lace patt to marker, sm, k2.

Cont in est patt for 5 (5, 13, 13, 13) more rows. End with WS row.

Inc row (RS): Sl1 wyif, M1L, k1, work in patt as set to last 2 sts, k1, M1R, k1. 119 (135, 151, 167, 183) sts.

Next row (WS): Sl 1 wyif, p2, work in patt to last 3 sts, p2, k1.

Work 6 (10, 14, 14, 14) more rows in patt as set.

Inc row (RS): Sl 1 wyif, M1L, k2, work in patt as set to last 3 sts, k2, M1R, k1. 121 (137, 153, 169, 185) sts.

Next row (WS): Sl 1 wyif, k1, p2, work in patt as set to last 3 sts, p2, k2.

Separate for Back and Front

Next row (RS): Sl 1 wyif, p1, k2, work in patt across 24 (28, 32, 36, 40) sts, pm to separate left front from back; work in patt to marked center st, p1, work in patt to last 28 (32, 36, 40, 44) sts; place them on holder or scrap yarn for left front.

back

With WS facing, k65 (73, 81, 89, 97) CO 14 (18, 18, 22, 26) sts for sleeve using twisted backward loop cast-on. Place rem 28 (32, 36, 40, 44) sts for right front on holder or scrap yarn. 79 (91, 99, 111, 123) sts.

Next row: K to end of row, CO 14 (18, 18, 22, 26) sts for second sleeve. 93 (109, 117, 133, 149) sts.

Knit 2 more rows.

Begin Madeira Lace Pattern

Row 1 and following WS rows: P46 (54, 58, 66, 74), pm, p1, pm, p46 (54, 58, 66, 74).

Row 2 and following RS rows: Sl 1, work Right-Slanting Madeira Lace to marker, k1, work Left-Slanting Madeira Lace to last st, k1.

Continue in Madeira Lace patt as set until piece measures approx 7 (8, 10, 11, 12)" from CO edge.

Knit 3 rows.

Place 35 (41, 44, 50, 56) sts for right sleeve and shoulder, 23 (27, 29, 33, 37) sts for back neck, and 35 (41, 44, 50, 56) sts for left sleeve and shoulder on separate holders or scrap yarn.

fronts

Right Front

With WS facing, transfer 28 (32, 36, 40, 44) sts for right front from holder or scrap yarn onto needle, join the new yarn at the armhole and k to end.

Next row (RS): K28 (32, 36, 40, 44), CO 14 (18, 18, 22, 26) sts using twisted backward loop cast-on. 42 (50, 54, 62, 70) sts.

Knit 2 rows.

Begin Madeira Lace Pattern

Row 1 and all WS rows: Sl 1 wyif, p to end.

Row 2 and all RS rows: Sl 1 wyif, work Left-Slanting Madeira Lace to end.

Work through 8 rows of Left-Slanting Madeira Lace a total of 2 (2, 3, 3, 4) times.

Purl 1 row.

Shape Neck

See decreasing information in the "Pattern Notes."

Next row (RS): BO 5 sts, work in patt as set to end. 37 (45, 49, 57, 65) sts.

Next row and all WS rows: Sl 1, purl to end.

Next row (RS): BO 2 sts, work in patt as set to end. 35 (43, 47, 55, 63) sts.

Dec every RS row by beg row with sl 1, ssk 0 (2, 3, 5, 7) times. 35 (41, 44, 50, 56) sts.

Work even in patt as set until piece measures approx 7 (8, 10, 11, 12)" from CO edge.

End with RS row.

Knit 1 row. Purl 1 row.

Place rem 35 (41, 44, 50, 56) sts for right sleeve and shoulder on holder or scrap yarn.

Left Front

With RS facing, transfer 28 (32, 36, 40, 44) sts for left front from holder or scrap yarn onto needle. Turn your knitting and join the new yarn at front center.

Next row (WS): K28 (32, 36, 40, 44), CO 14 (18, 18, 22, 26) sts using twisted backward loop cast-on. 42 (50, 54, 62, 70) sts.

Knit 3 rows.

Cut yarn. Slide sts to other end. Join yarn at sleeve end.

Begin Madeira Lace Pattern

Row 1 and all WS rows: Sl 1 wyif, p to end.

Row 2 and all RS rows: Sl 1 wyif, work Right-Slanting Madeira Lace to end.

Work 8 rows of Right-Slanting Madeira Lace a total of 2 (2, 3, 3, 4) times.

Purl 1 row.

Shape Neck

Next row (WS): BO 5 sts, p to end. 37 (45, 49, 57, 65) sts.

Next row (RS): Sl 1 wyif, work in patt as set to end.

Next row (WS): BO 2 sts, p to end. 35 (43, 47, 55, 63) sts.

Begin decreases on RS rows.

Dec every RS row by ending with k2tog 0 (2, 3, 5, 7) times. 35 (41, 44, 50, 56) sts.

Work even in patt as set until piece measures approx 7 (8, 10, 11, 12)" from CO edge.

End with RS row.

Knit 1 row. Purl 1 row.

Place rem 35 (41, 44, 50, 56) sts for left sleeve and shoulder on holder or scrap yarn.

finishing

Weave in loose ends.

Block to measurements.

With RS tog, join shoulders using three-needle bind-off (see the "Special Knitting Techniques" appendix). Block seams.

sleeve trim

With RS facing, join yarn and pick up and knit 42 (46, 55, 60, 65) sts along sleeve edge.

Knit 3 rows. BO all sts.

Sew underarm seam.

Rep for second sleeve.

button band (left front)

NOTE Due to possibility of gauge difference, make sure to measure length of bands as you work on them.

Transfer 3 (3, 4, 4, 5) sts from holder or scrap yarn to needle.

Work in garter st until length of button band reaches 1" before Madeira Lace. With RS facing, k3 (3, 4, 4, 5), CO 3 (3, 4, 4, 3) sts using twisted backward loop cast-on. 6 (6, 8, 8, 8) sts.

Cont working in garter st until piece measures 5.5 (6, 8.5, 9.5, 10.5)" from CO edge or reaches neckline. BO all sts. Sew band to left front.

buttonhole band (right front)

Transfer 3 (3, 4, 4, 5) sts from scrap yarn to needle.

Work in garter st until length of buttonhole band reaches 1" before Madeira Lace. With WS facing, k3 (3, 4, 4, 5), CO 3 (3, 4, 4, 3) sts using twisted backward loop cast-on. 6 (6, 8, 8, 8) sts.

Knit 6 (6, 6, 8, 10) rows.

Next row (RS): K2, BO 2 (2, 4, 4, 4) sts, k2.

Next row: K2, CO 2 (2, 4, 4, 4) sts, k2.

Knit 16 rows.

Next row (RS): K2, BO 2 (2, 4, 4, 4) sts, k2.

Next row: K2, CO 2 (2, 4, 4, 4) sts, k2.

For sizes 6, 8, and 10 only:

Knit 16 rows.

Next row (RS): K2, BO 2 (2, 4, 4, 4) sts, k2.

Next row: K2, CO 2 (2, 4, 4, 4) sts, k2.

For all sizes:

Knit 6 (6, 6, 8, 10) rows.

BO all sts. Sew band to right front.

neckline trim

With RS facing, join yarn at right front neck edge. Pick up and knit 16 (16, 18, 18, 20) sts from right front, k23 (27, 29, 33, 37) sts held for back neck, pick up and knit 16 (16, 18, 18, 20) sts from left front. 55 (59, 65, 69, 77) sts.

Knit 4 rows. BO all sts.

Sew on buttons. Block trims.

RONIA
short-sleeved
cardigan

RONIA
short-sleeved cardigan

by linda wilgus

Ronia is a sweet short-sleeved cardigan that knits up quickly in a worsted-weight cotton blend. The lace panels down the front, empire-waist shaping, and slightly puffed sleeves combine for a wonderfully girly top that would be perfect paired with jeans or thrown over a summer dress on a cooler day. Knit from the top down, Ronia is entirely seamless, and the lace panels are easy to work, even if you've never tried lace before.

pattern notes

This cardigan is knit from the top down, working back and forth on a circular needle, with raglan increases.

The chart in this pattern is available for download at www.wiley.com/go/moreknittinginthesun.

directions
yoke

Using circular needle, CO 64 (68, 68, 68, 74, 74) sts. *Do not join.* Beg with RS row, work 3 rows in k2, p2 rib.

Raglan Set-up Row
Next row (WS): Continuing in k2, p2 rib, work 12 (13, 13, 13, 14, 14) sts, place marker (pm), work 8 sts, pm, work 24 (26, 26, 26, 30, 30) sts, pm, work 8 sts, pm, work to end.

Begin Raglan Shaping and Lace Panels
Row 1 (RS): *K to 1 st before marker, kfb, slip marker (sm), kfb, rep from * 3 times, k to end. 8 sts inc'd. 72 (76, 76, 76, 82, 82) sts.

SIZE
2 (4, 6, 8, 10, 12)

FINISHED MEASUREMENTS
Chest circumference: 22.5 (25, 26.5, 28.5, 30, 32)"

Length: 14 (15, 16, 18, 20, 22)"

MATERIALS
- Cascade *Sierra* (80% pima cotton, 20% wool; 191 yd. per 100g skein); color: 05; 2 (3, 3, 4, 4, 5) skeins
- US 7 (4.5mm) circular needle, 29" or longer (*or size needed to match gauge*)
- US 7 (4.5mm) double-pointed needles

continued ➤

➤ **continued**

- 4 stitch markers, including 3 removable
- Stitch holders or scrap yarn
- 3 buttons, 0.75" diameter
- Tapestry needle

GAUGE

18 sts × 24 rows = 4" in St st, unblocked

SKILLS USED

Basic increasing and decreasing, knitting from the top down, simple lace pattern, cable cast-on

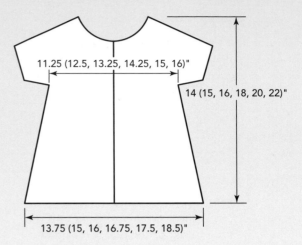

11.25 (12.5, 13.25, 14.25, 15, 16)"

14 (15, 16, 18, 20, 22)"

13.75 (15, 16, 16.75, 17.5, 18.5)"

Ronia Lace Chart

	5	4	3	2	1	
4						
						3
2						
	○	●	⚠	●	○	1

Key to Ronia Lace Chart

☐ RS: knit stitch
WS: purl stitch

● RS: purl stitch
WS: knit stitch

○ yarn over

⚠ purl 3 together

Row 2 (WS): Purl.

Row 3: K3, yo, p1, p3tog, p1, yo, *k to 1 st before marker, kfb, sm, kfb, rep from * 3 times, work to last 8 sts, yo, p1, p3tog, p1, yo, k3. 8 sts inc'd. 80 (84, 84, 84, 90, 90) sts.

Row 4: Purl.

Rep these 4 rows 5 (6, 7, 8, 8, 9) times, then rep Rows 1 and 2 once. 168 (188, 204, 220, 226, 242) sts.

Divide Sleeves and Body

Next row (RS): K3, yo, p1, p3tog, p1, yo, *k to marker and remove it, place next 34 (38, 42, 46, 46, 50) sts on a holder or scrap yarn for sleeve, remove marker, rep from * once, k to last 8 sts, yo, p1, p3tog, p1, yo, k3. 100 (112, 120, 128, 134, 142) sts on needle.

body

Work 2 rows in rev St st (knit 1 row, purl 1 row).

Next row (WS): Purl, inc 24 sts evenly spaced across row. 124 (136, 144, 152, 158, 166) sts.

Row 1 (RS): K3, yo, p1, p3tog, p1, yo, k to last 8 sts, yo, p1, p3tog, p1, yo, k3.

Row 2 (WS): Purl.

Row 3: Knit.

Row 4: Purl.

Rep these 4 rows until work measures 13.5 (14.5, 15.5, 17.5, 19.5, 21.5)" from CO edge.

Work 4 rows in k2, p2 rib.

BO in rib.

sleeves

Transfer 34 (38, 42, 46, 46, 50) sts held for sleeve to dpns, attach yarn and join to work in the round.

Increase 4 sts in each of the next 4 rounds as follows:

Round 1: K4 (6, 8, 10, 10, 12), *m1, k9, rep from * twice, m1, k to end.

Round 2: K4 (6, 8, 10, 10, 12), *m1, k10, rep from * twice, m1, k to end.

Round 3: K3 (5, 7, 9, 9, 11), *m1, k12, rep from * twice, m1, k to end.

Round 4: K3 (4, 6, 8, 8, 10), *m1, k14, rep from * twice, m1, k to end. 50 (54, 58, 62, 62, 66) sts.

Next round: K1 (3, 5, 7, 7, 9), (k2tog) 22 times, k to end. 28 (32, 36, 40, 40, 44) sts.

Work 4 rows in k2, p2 rib.

BO in rib.

Rep for second sleeve.

button bands

Using circular needle, pick up and knit 54 (58, 62, 70, 78, 86) sts from top to bottom along left front.

Work 4 rows in k2, p2 rib.

BO in rib.

Pick up and knit 54 (58, 62, 70, 78, 86) sts from bottom to top along right front.

Row 1: Work k2, p2 rib.

Place 3 removable markers or pins for buttonhole placement: the first 4 sts from top, the second 4 sts above the rev St st band, and the third halfway between these two.

Row 2: *Work in rib to marker, sm, BO 2 sts, rep from * twice, work to end.

Row 3: *Work in rib to BO sts from last row, CO 2 sts using cable cast-on (see the "Special Knitting Techniques" appendix), rep from * 2 times, work to end.

Row 4: Work in rib.

BO in rib.

finishing

Attach buttons to buttonband opposite buttonholes. Weave in ends. Block cardigan.

special knitting techniques

cast-ons

Backward Loop Cast-On

This cast-on is also called the *single cast-on* or the *backward-e cast-on*. You typically use this cast-on when you need to add stitches in the middle of a piece, and you will use just one needle.

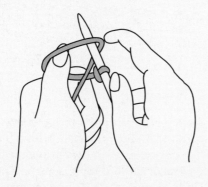

1. Make a slipknot and place it on the RH needle, or, if you are in the middle of a piece, turn the work, and hold the needle in your right hand.
2. Wrap the working yarn once around your left thumb with the yarn attached to the needle on the top and the yarn attached to the ball on the bottom.
3. Insert the needle into the thumb loop and slip it onto the needle.
4. Repeat steps 2 and 3 until you've cast on the appropriate number of stitches.

Cable Cast-On

1. Make a slipknot and place it on the LH needle.
2. With the second needle, knit into this stitch, but do not slip the stitch off the needle. Instead, transfer this new stitch onto the LH needle.

3. Insert the RH needle *between* the last 2 stitches on the LH needle.
4. Wrap the yarn and pull the new stitch through, just as you do when knitting. Transfer the new stitch to the LH needle.
5. Repeat steps 3 and 4 until you have cast on the correct number of stitches.

Knitted Cast-On

1. Make a slipknot and place it on the LH needle.

2. With the second needle, knit into this stitch, but do not slip the stitch off the needle. Instead, transfer this new stitch onto the LH needle.

3. Repeat step 2 until you have cast on the appropriate number of stitches.

Longtail Cast-On

Before you begin the longtail cast-on, you need to estimate how long to make your tail. You can conservatively figure an inch per stitch, or approximately 4 times wider than whatever you are making (if your sweater is 20" across, you'll want a tail about 80" long). You will only use one needle. (Some knitters like to cast on around both needles held together and then pull one out at the end. This ensures that the cast-on edge is tidy, but not too tight.)

1. Make a slipknot and place it on the RH needle.

2. Hold the tail end with your left hand and the working yarn in your right hand.

3. Wrap the working yarn once around your left thumb.

4. Insert the needle into the thumb loop, but leave it on your thumb.

5. Wrap the yarn in your right hand around the needle.

6. Bring the needle through the loop on your thumb and move it toward you. Then gently snug up the stitch.

7. Repeat steps 3–6 until you've cast on the appropriate number of stitches.

Provisional Cast-On, Crochet Method

You may use any provisional cast-on you like throughout this book, but this is my preferred method.

1. Make a slip knot with scrap yarn and place on crochet hook.

2. Hold crochet hook above the needle, *wrap yarn around under the needle and then wrap yarn over crochet hook and pull it through the stitch on the hook*. There is 1 stitch on the needle and 1 stitch on the hook.

3. Repeat from * to * until you have the appropriate number of stitches on the needle.

4. When you have cast on the correct number of sts, cut yarn and pull tail through final st on crochet hook; put a knot at this end of yarn to mark the end that you will later use to begin unraveling the chain.

5. Begin knitting with the main yarn as the pattern describes.

When you need to remove the provisional cast-on, unravel the crochet chain starting at the marked end. Carefully place each of the live stitches exposed on a needle and begin working.

decreases

S2KP: (A centered double decrease.) Slip 2 stitches as if to k2tog. Knit 1 stitch. Pass the 2 slipped stitches over the stitch just knit.
SK2P: (A left-leaning double decrease.) Slip 1 stitch, k2tog, pass the slipped stitch over the stitch just made.
K3TOG: (A right-leaning double decrease.) Knit 3 stitches together as 1 stitch.

increases

kfb (Knit in the front and the back of the next stitch.) Knit the next stitch normally, but do not slide it off the LH needle. Insert the RH needle into the back of the same stitch, behind the LH needle. Wrap the yarn and pull it through. Move both new stitches off the LH needle.

pfb: (Purl in the front and the back of the next stitch.) Purl the next stitch normally, but do not slide it off the LH needle. Insert the RH needle into the back of the same stitch by bringing it around in a U-turn and inserting the needle from left to right. Purl this stitch and then move both new stitches off the LH needle.

M1: Make 1 increases are increases that are made between 2 stitches. There are two variations: one slants a bit to the left (M1L), the other a bit to the right (M1R). If a pattern does not specify M1L or M1R, choose whichever one you find easiest to work.

M1L (Make 1 Left): Lift the horizontal thread between stitches by inserting the left needle from front to back. Knit into the back of this stitch.

M1R (Make 1 Right): Lift the horizontal thread between stitches by inserting the left needle from back to front. Knit into the front of this stitch.

M1P (Make 1 Purl): Lift the horizontal thread between stitches by inserting the left needle from back to front. Purl into the front of this stitch.

RLI (Right Lifted Increase): Insert the RH needle into the stitch just below the first stitch on the LH needle, knit it, then knit the stitch on the LH needle.

LLI (Left Lifted Increase): Knit the stitch on the needle, then with the LH needle pick up the stitch two rows below the stitch on the needle and knit it.

Yarn Overs

YO (before a knit stitch): Bring yarn to the front of the work, between the needles. Work the next stitch as specified, which will bring the yarn up over the needle creating an eyelet and an extra stitch.

YO2: (A double yarn over.) Bring the yarn to the front between the needles. Wrap the yarn around the right needle once, bringing it back to the front of the work. Work the next stitch as specified. Individual patterns will describe whether you are to treat the double yarn over as 2 stitches or 1 stitch in the next row.

i-cord

I-cord is a skinny tube of knitting that is perfect for handles, straps, and ties. Use 2 double-pointed needles to make I-cord.

1. Cast on the specified number of stitches.
2. Knit the stitches on the needle, do not turn the work.
3. Slide the stitches to the other end of the needle, bringing the yarn snugly across the back of the work.
4. Repeat steps 2 and 3 until your I-cord is long enough.

i-cord bind-off

1. Cast on 3 additional sts to LH needle (or as pattern directs).
2. Using a dpn, k2, ssk (using the last of the 3 sts and 1 st from the edge of the garment).
3. Slip 3 sts back to LH needle, do not turn.
4. Repeat steps 2 and 3 until only 3 sts remain. Bind off or continue as pattern directs.

attached i-cord

Work the same as the I-cord bind-off above, picking up stitches around the finished edge of the piece as you go to complete the ssk.

picking up stitches (pick up and knit)

1. Working from right to left with the RS facing, insert the needle through the edge of the knitted work, working in the first row of complete stitches along the tops of pieces or in the ladder between stitches along the sides of pieces.

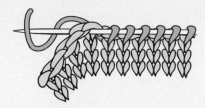

2. Wrap the needle as if to knit (or purl) and pull the loop through to the RS.

3. Repeat steps 1 and 2, spacing your stitches evenly as described in the pattern.

whipstitch

1. Place your pieces WS up with the two edges to be sewn aligned and parallel to you. Thread a length of yarn onto a tapestry needle. Work from right to left (for right handers), and keep the needle always pointing the same way, toward your left hip.

2. Insert the needle through one stitch on the upper piece then one stitch on the lower piece. Draw the yarn through.

3. Repeat this step until your seam is complete.

mattress stitch

Lay your two pieces RS up with the two edges to be sewn next to each other. Thread a length of yarn onto a tapestry needle.

1. Work in the "ladder" between the edge st and the next st on the sides of pieces. Work in the sts in the row below the bind-off for the tops of pieces.

2. Insert the needle under the first 2 rungs on the ladder (or the 2 legs of the first st) on the RH piece, and back up. Draw the yarn through.

3. Go under the first 2 rungs (or the 2 legs of the st on the LH piece) and back up. Draw the yarn through.

4. Go in to the RH piece where the yarn emerged and under 2 rungs (or 1 stitch).

5. Go in to the LH piece where the yarn emerged and under 2 rungs (or 1 stitch).

6. Continue in this manner, using 1 rung or 1 leg of a stitch as needed to ease the fit between the two pieces as needed. Grasp the two ends of the sewing yarn and pull gently to snug the pieces into place.

grafting (Kitchener stitch)

A method of joining two pieces almost invisibly by mimicking a row of knitting with a tapestry needle. With right sides facing, place the pieces to be joined on a surface, each on its own needle, with the needles parallel to one another. Thread a tapestry needle with the working yarn.

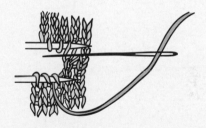

1. Insert the needle into the first stitch on the bottom needle as if to purl. Pull the yarn through. Leave the stitch on the needle.

2. Insert the needle into the first stitch on the top needle as if to knit. Pull the yarn through. Leave the stitch on the needle.

3. Insert the needle into the first stitch on the bottom needle again, but this time as if to knit. Slip the stitch off the knitting needle.

4. Insert the needle into the next stitch on the bottom needle as if to purl and leave it on the needle.

5. Insert the needle into the first stitch on the top needle again, this time as if to purl, and slip it off the needle.

6. Insert the needle into the next stitch on the top needle, as if to knit. Leave this stitch on the needle.

7. Repeat steps 3–6 until all the stitches have been joined and slipped off the needle. *Remember, you will always go into a stitch twice.*

three-needle bind-off

The three-needle bind-off is used to join two pieces together without seaming. Put each set of stitches on a separate knitting needle. Hold the needles parallel in the left hand with right sides together and wrong sides facing out.

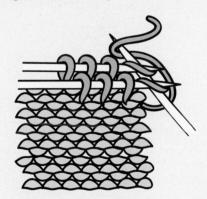

1. Insert a third needle (of the same size or slightly larger than the working needles) into the first stitch on the front needle and then the first stitch on the back needle. Knit these 2 stitches together.

2. Knit the next stitch on the front needle and the next stitch on the back needle together as in step 1.

3. Bring the outside stitch on the RH needle up over the inside stitch on the RH needle as you do to bind off.

4. Repeat steps 2 and 3 until all the stitches are bound off. Cut yarn and pull through the last loop to secure.

wrap & turn (w&t)

To add partial rows (or *short rows*) to create shaping, you have to turn around in the middle of a row. To do so without creating a hole, you must "wrap" the turning stitches as follows:

1. Work to the specified stitch in the pattern. Slip the next stitch to the RH needle.

2. Bring yarn to the opposite side of the work.

3. Slip the stitch back to the LH needle.

4. Turn your work and bring the yarn to the correct position to work this next row.

5. Repeat these 4 steps as described in the pattern.

When you encounter a wrapped stitch in subsequent rows:

1. Slip the wrapped stitch onto the RH needle.

2. Insert the LH needle into the wrap at the base of the stitch from bottom to top.

3. Slip the wrapped stitch back to the LH needle.

4. Knit (or purl) the wrap and the stitch together.

crochet techniques
Chain Stitch (ch)

1. Make a slipknot for the first stitch if you do not already have a stitch on the hook.

2. Wrap the yarn around the hook from back to front and catch it with the end of the hook.

3. Bring this loop through the stitch on the hook. There is 1 loop on the hook.

4. Repeat steps 2 and 3 for each chain stitch required.

Slip Stitch (Crochet)

You will have 1 loop on the hook to begin. If you do not, insert the hook into the first stitch, wrap the yarn around the hook, and pull a loop through.

1. Insert the hook into the next stitch as the pattern directs from front to back.

2. Wrap the yarn over the hook and pull the loop through the stitch and the loop on the hook. One loop remains on the hook.

3. Repeat steps 1 and 2 for each slip stitch.

Single Crochet (sc)

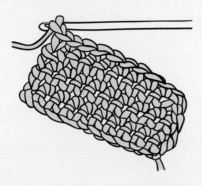

You will have 1 loop on the hook to begin.

1. Insert the hook into the work as the pattern directs.

2. Wrap the yarn around the hook and pull it through the work. There are 2 loops on the hook.

3. Wrap the yarn and pull it through 2 loops. There is 1 loop on the hook.

4. Repeat steps 1–3 for each single crochet.

Half Double Crochet (hdc)

You will have 1 loop on the hook to begin.

1. Wrap the yarn over the hook.

2. Insert the hook into the next st to be worked.

3. Wrap the yarn over the hook and pull the yarn through the stitch. There are 3 loops on the hook.

4. Wrap the yarn over the hook and pull through all 3 loops. One loop remains on the hook.

5. Repeat steps 1–4 for each half double crochet.

Double Crochet (dc)

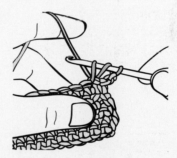

You will have 1 loop on the hook to begin.

1. Wrap the yarn around the hook.

2. Insert the hook into the work as the pattern directs.

3. Wrap the yarn around the hook and pull it through the work. There are 3 loops on the hook.

4. Wrap the yarn around the hook and pull it through the first 2 loops on the hook. There are now 2 loops on the hook.

5. Wrap the yarn around the hook and pull it through the remaining 2 loops. There is 1 loop on the hook.

6. Repeat steps 1–5 for each double crochet.

knitting abbreviations

Abbreviation	Meaning
alt	alternate
beg	begin(ning)
BO	bind off (cast off)
CC	contrasting color
Ch	chain stitch (crochet)
CO	cast on
cont	continue(ing)
dc	double crochet
dec	decrease(ing)
dpn(s)	double-pointed needle(s)
foll	follow(s)(ing)
g	grams
hdc	half double crochet
inc	increase(ing)
k	knit
k tbl	knit through back loop
k2tog	knit 2 sts together (right-leaning decrease)
k2tog tbl	knit 2 sts together through the back loops (left-leaning decrease)
k3tog	knit 3 sts together (right-leaning double decrease)
k3tog tbl	knit 3 sts together through the back loops (left-leaning double decrease)
kfb	knit into front and back of stitch (increase)
LH	left hand
LLI	left lifted increase
m	meter(s)
M1	make 1 (increase between stitches)
M1L	make 1 left
M1R	make 1 right
M1P	make 1 purl
MC	main color
mm	millimeters
p	purl
p2tog	purl 2 sts together (decrease)
p2tog tbl	purl 2 sts together through back loop (decrease)
p3tog	purl 3 sts together

Abbreviation	Meaning
patt(s)	pattern(s)
pfb	purl into front and back of stitch (increase)
pm	place marker
psso	pass slipped stitch(es) over
rem	remaining
rep	repeat
rev St st	reverse stockinette stitch
RH	right hand
RLI	right lifted increase
RS	right side(s)
s2kp	slip 2 sts as if to k2tog, k1, pass the slipped sts over
sc	single crochet
sk2p	slip 1 st, k2tog, pass slipped st over
skp	slip 1 st as if to knit, k1, pass the slipped st over
sl	slip (slip sts purlwise, unless directed otherwise)
sl st	slip stitch
sm	slip marker
ssk	slip 2 sts as if to knit, one at a time, then k those 2 sts together
ssp	slip 2 sts as if to purl, one at a time, then p those 2 sts together
st(s)	stitch(es)
St st	stockinette stitch
tbl	through back of loop(s)
tog	together
w&t	wrap and turn
WS	wrong side(s)
wyib	with yarn in back
wyif	with yarn in front
yd.	yard(s)
YO	yarn over
YO2	yarn over twice
* *	repeat directions between *s as indicated
[ ]	repeat directions within brackets as many times as indicated

Learn more about the highlighted terms in the "Special Knitting Techniques" appendix.

contributing
designers

Sarah Barbour
Sarah Barbour lives in Urbana, Illinois, where the summers are hot and the winters are cold—which means it's always perfect for knitting! She has been designing professionally for five years and teaches knitting and crochet classes at several local venues. The rest of the time, she's a stay-at-home mother to three little girls. You can find her on Ravelry as Rope and see more of her patterns at www.ropeknits.com.

Tian Connaughton
Tian lives in rural western Massachusetts with her husband, son, two cats, chickens, and a duck. After a long day at the office and an hour-long commute home, she usually tucks herself away in her craft room knitting, crocheting, or spinning. She believes that she owes her sanity to her family and crafty life. You can find more of her patterns and craft-related adventures on her blog at tian-knitdesigns.blogspot.com.

Beautia Dew
Beautia is a self-taught knitter and freelance designer who lives in Pittsburgh, Pennsylvania. Her designs have been featured in a number of web magazines, including *Knitty*, *The Fibertarian*, and *Tangled*. You can find her patterns at B. Girl B. Knits (http://bgirlbknits.blogspot.com/).

Carol Feller
Carol Feller is an independent knitwear designer living in Cork, Ireland, with her husband and four little boys. Trained as both an artist and a structural engineer, she has found a real "home" in knitting and design, which allow her to combine the best of both these worlds. Carol's patterns have been widely published in books and magazines (*Interweave Knits*, *Knitty*, *Knitting in the Sun*, and *Yarn Forward*). To see her self-published patterns, visit www.stolenstitches.com. Watch for her upcoming book, *Contemporary Irish Knitting*, which will be published by Wiley in the fall of 2011.

Katya Frankel
Katya is a freelance knitwear designer, living and working in Newcastle upon Tyne, England. Surrounded by crafts of all kinds during her childhood, knitting and design come naturally to Katya. She draws design inspirations from the world around her: nature, art, people, and books as well as yarns. Her design philosophy combines elegant and simple silhouettes with arresting design elements in classic, wearable designs. Her designs have appeared in publications such as *Yarn Forward* and *Interweave Knits*. You can find out more about her work at www.katyafrankel.com.

Mary Gildersleeve

Mary Gildersleeve taught herself to knit at age eight and has been designing ever since (including patterns in *Knitters*, *Cast On*, and as an independent designer for Knit Picks). She is a published writer *(Great Yarns for the Close-Knit Family* and *In His Image: Nurturing Creativity in the Heart of Your Home)*, reviewer, and teacher. She enjoys talking about knitting whenever anyone will listen. She is married with five children. You can find out more about Mary on her blog at http://livingknitting.blogspot.com/.

Faina Goberstein

Faina Goberstein is fascinated by endless possibilities of various knitting techniques and stitch patterns. When she is not designing, she enjoys teaching mathematics, traveling, and fine arts. She lives in California and blogs at http://fainasknittingmode.blogspot.com/. Faina is co-author of *Casual, Elegant Knits* and her work has been featured in many publications, most recently *Interweave Knits*, *Interweave Crochet*, *Knitscene*, *Twist Collective*, and *Knitting in the Sun*.

Tabetha Hedrick

When Tabetha Hedrick learned to knit, the idea of entering the precarious world of design was a foreign one. But with encouragement from family and friends, it has become a passionate path of her existence. She believes that fiber equals ecstasy. When not entertaining her two daughters, Tabetha exploits her perfectionist nature as she knits and designs. You can follow her knitting exploits at www.piscesknits.blogspot.com or on Ravelry (username is tabismiles).

Talitha Kuomi

Talitha spends part of her yearly family vacation literally "knitting in the sun" on the beach or sitting on the screened porch with the ocean breeze skimming across her toes. Her work has been published in *Interweave Knits and Knitscene,* as well as the online mags *Petite Purls* (www.petitepurls.com) and *Tangled* (www.tangledness.com). She sells patterns and writes about her adventures at www.talithakuomi.com. Stop by and say "hello."

Janine Le Cras

Janine Le Cras lives and works on the beautiful island of Guernsey in the middle of the English Channel. The island's natural beauty is a constant inspiration for her designs. Janine's designs are featured in several books and magazines and she is currently a designer-in-residence for the Unique Sheep. You can find her on Ravelry as Guernseygal.

Anne Lecrivain

Anne has been sewing and crocheting since age eight. She officially picked up the pointy sticks three years later, but has only been knitting seriously for the last ten years. Knitting has taken hold over her need to express herself creatively. She lives a blissful life while knitting and teaching at Anacapa Fine Yarns (http://anacapafineyarns.com/) and making knitted luxuries for loved ones. You can find her lazily blogging along at http://moonlightstitches.blogspot.com/ or on Ravelry as anneland22.

Lisa Limber

Lisa Limber has been knitting for thirty-six years. After many years in the corporate world, she now makes her living as a knitwear designer, yarn rep, and by teaching knitting workshops throughout Southern California. Her designs are inspired by the textures and colors of the yarns she uses. Lisa's website is gourmetknits.com, and her Ravelry name is also gourmetknits. When she is not working, her knitting time is spent with Zoe, her Cairn Terrier.

Anne Kuo Lukito

Anne fell into designing soon after she taught herself to knit. Her works have been published in *Knitty, Interweave Knits, Knitscene, Twist Collective,* and several books, including *Knitting in the Sun.* She lives in Southern California with her husband and spoiled, fat cats. If it wasn't for bouts of insomnia, Anne would never find time to knit or use up her abundance of creative energy. Or is it the other way around? Anne's patterns, tutorials, and blog can be found on her website, www.crafty diversions.com.

Laura Nelkin

Laura *loves* to knit and splits her work hours between her own knitwear pattern company, Nelkin Designs (www.nelkindesigns.com), and her paying gig as the design director at Schaefer Yarn Company (www.schaeferyarn. com). After working, designing, publishing, and traveling to teach, there aren't many hours left in the day, so she spends the rest of her time plotting to take long vacations with her family so she can play and knit some more!

Kendra Nitta

Kendra Nitta knits and designs with a focus on silk and plant-based fibers. Since 2007, her patterns have appeared in over a dozen books and magazines, most recently in *Sock Yarn One-Skein Wonders, Beyond Toes: Knitting Adventures with Judy's Magic Cast-On, 1000 Fabulous Knit Hats, Blossom Street Collection Book 1, Knitcircus,* and *Interweave Knits Holiday Gifts.* Follow her knitting, sewing, and designing adventures at www.missknitta.com.

Kate Oates

Kate Oates is the designer for Tot Toppers (www.tottoppers.com). She enjoys designing hats in particular, as well as garments for babies and children. Her projects often reflect a whimsical spirit. She has recently started a new line for those of us who are not tots, called *When I Grow Up.* Kate also strives to add knitting patterns for boys because she has two of her own! When she can pull herself away from her knitting, she is finishing up a PhD in Political Science from the University of Florida. Her blog is located at www.tottoppers.com and she keeps a constant eye on her Ravelry group for pattern support.

Susan Robicheau

Susan Robicheau is a freelance designer living in Nova Scotia, Canada, where the temperatures can soar during the summer months. At age six, Susan began learning how to design and knit clothes for her dolls. She has created designs for *Creative Knitting, Crochet! Magazine, Leisure Arts,* and *House of White Birches.* She is the author of *Bright & Cheery Knit Dishcloths.*

Lisa S. Rowe

Lisa is mom to three active kids, so she knows the kinds of knitwear that kids want to wear. She's been knitting for over twenty years. Her patterns have been featured in *Interweave Knits* and *Knitter's Magazine.* She has also designed for Classic Elite's *Curvy Knits* and Reynolds. You can find her on Ravelry as Spinsterrowe.

Carol J. Sulcoski

Carol is a former attorney turned knitting designer and hand-dyer. She is author of *Knitting Socks With Handpainted Yarns* and co-author of *Knit So Fine: Designs with Skinny Yarn* (both published by Interweave Press). Her work has been published in *Vogue Knitting, KnitSimple, St-Denis Magazine,* and *KnitScene.* She also founded Black Bunny Fibers (www. blackbunnyfibers.com), an independent dyeing business that creates unique handpainted yarns and fibers. You can find her indie patterns on Ravelry and Patternfish.

Stacey Trock

Stacey Trock is a knitting and crochet designer living in New Haven, Connecticut. She is the author of *Cuddly Crochet: Adorable Hats, Toys, and More,* and is the amigurumi designer for FreshStitches (freshstitches.com). She has a soft spot for children, and her designs are typically suited for the little ones in this world. When she's not holding yarn, Stacey blogs about knitting, crocheting, designing, and traveling at www.freshstitches.com/wordpress. The remaining hours in her day are spent living a very domesticated life, with the goal of self-sufficiency always on the horizon.

Julie Turjoman

Julie Turjoman is the author of *Brave New Knits: 26 Projects and Personalities From the Knitting Blogosphere.* She lives in the San Francisco Bay area, where she blogs about knitting and other sundry fascinations at www.julieturjoman.com.

Katherine Vaughan

Katherine Vaughan has been knitting for over twenty-five years and designing for more than five years. She primarily designs kidswear and accessories for adults and the home, particularly in non-wool yarns. She daylights as a medical librarian in North Carolina, where it is (almost) never too hot to knit. Her online home is http://www.ktlvdesigns.com.

Linda Wilgus

Linda Wilgus lives in Virginia Beach with her husband, daughter, and sock-stealing Golden Retriever. Every three years, they move to a different place in the world, courtesy of the U.S. Navy. Linda loves designing seamless knits for adults, children, and babies. She draws inspiration from current as well as vintage fashion, yarn itself, and the different places that she has lived. Her designs regularly appear in books and magazines and have been featured online in *Knitty.* See more of her designs on her website, woollymammothknits.com, or find her on Ravelry as linw.

yarn sources

The following companies have generously provided the yarns used for the samples seen in *More Knitting in the Sun*. Find out more about these companies and where you can find their products through the websites listed below, or visit your local yarn shop for help selecting yarns for these projects.

Alchemy Yarns of Transformation
www.alchemyyarns.com

Artful Yarns (JCA)
www.jcacrafts.com

Berroco
berroco.com

Cascade Yarns
www.cascadeyarns.com

Classic Elite Yarns
www.classiceliteyarns.com

Crystal Palace Yarns
www.straw.com

Debbie Bliss
www.debbieblissonline.com
www.knittingfever.com (U.S. distributor)

Frog Tree Yarns
www.frogtreeyarns.com

Knit Picks
www.knitpicks.com

Hemp for Knitting
www.lanaknits.com

Lion Brand Yarns
www.lionbrand.com

Louet North America
www.louet.com

Madelinetosh
madelinetosh.com

Naturally Caron
www.naturallycaron.com

Punta Yarns
www.puntayarns.com

Rowan
www.knitrowan.com

Schaefer
www.schaeferyarn.com

Spud & Chloë
www.spudandchloe.com

Sublime (KFI)
www.knittingfever.com

Zitron (Skacel Collection, Inc)
www.skacelknitting.com

index

about the author

Kristi Porter is an author, designer, technical editor, and teacher. In addition to authoring *Knitting in the Sun* (Wiley Publishing, Inc., 2009), *Knitting for Dogs* (Simon & Schuster, 2005), and *Knitting Patterns For Dummies* (Wiley Publishing, Inc., 2007), her work has been featured in the *Knitgrrl* series, the *Big Girl Knits* series, *No Sheep for You,* and *KnitWit.* She has been a contributor to *Knitty.com* since its start in 2002.

As a knitting instructor and mother in Southern California, Kristi knows well what will appeal to children and warm-weather knitters. Choosing projects and guiding her students in creating garments that they will enjoy knitting—and their children and grandchildren will enjoy wearing—has helped her understand the need for designs specifically created for warmer climates.

Kristi doesn't remember learning to knit as a child, but she captured the basics and an enthusiasm for the craft from her mother, her aunt, and her grandmother and has been knitting ever since. Her girls have picked up the basics of knitting, too, so the tradition of three generations of knitters in her family continues.

Kristi designs and teaches in sunny La Jolla, California, where she makes her home with her husband and two daughters.